THE INDIAN IN AMERICAN LIFE

BY G. E. E. LINDQUIST

WITH THE COLLABORATION OF
ERNA GUNTHER · JOHN H. HOLST
AND FLORA WARREN SEYMOUR

Foreword by

MARK A. DAWBER

FRIENDSHIP PRESS
NEW YORK

THE REVEREND G. E. E. LINDQUIST, D.D., after a wide experience as teacher, missionary, Y.M.C.A. secretary, and director of religious education among the American Indians, became in 1927 Field Secretary of the Society for Propagating the Gospel among the Indians and Others in North America. In this capacity he has increasingly served missionary agencies of many denominations in surveying their Indian work and planning their programs of action. He was appointed in 1930 by President Hoover a member of the Board of Indian Commissioners. Dr. Lindquist represents the Home Missions Council of North America in many of its contacts on the field. He was the founder of the National Fellowship of Indian Workers and is its secretary. Among his books are *The Red Man in the United States* and *The Jesus Road and the Red Man.*

ERNA GUNTHER, Ph.D., took her doctor's degree in anthropology at Columbia University and is Professor of Anthropology at the University of Washington as well as Director of the Washington State Museum, Seattle. She has made field studies among the Indians both in the Southwest and Northwest and is the author of several works embodying the results of this research.

JOHN H. HOLST, M.A., is an educator of long experience. For many years he was Director of the School of Agriculture and head of the Department of Psychology and Teacher Training at the State College of the University of Montana. From 1928 to his retirement in 1943 he was a Supervisor of Indian Schools under the Office of Indian Affairs.

FLORA WARREN SEYMOUR, LL.M., is a lawyer, traveler, and author whose lifelong study of Indians and the history of the West has resulted in an extended list of books. Some of Mrs. Seymour's best-known volumes are *The Story of the Red Man, Indian Agents of the Old Frontier,* and *Women of Trail and Wigwam.* She spent six years in the United States Indian Service and was the first woman appointed by the President to serve on the Board of Indian Commissioners.

THIS BOOK HAS BEEN MANUFACTURED IN COMPLIANCE WITH ORDERS OF THE WAR PRODUCTION BOARD FOR CONSERVING PAPER AND OTHER MATERIALS.

Printed in the United States of America

CONTENTS

FOREWORD

by Mark A. Dawber

Executive Secretary, Home Missions Council of North America

In these times when we are being made to think in global dimensions, when our reading forces us to look at our world as "One World," and when we are being constantly reminded of the international and interracial implications of the war, why, some may ask, should we stop to read about the American Indians, one of the smallest numerical groups in our population?

The answer is simple and very reasonable. It is that unless we can hope to make possible to the American Indian the things we say we are fighting for in the world, *for* the world, then our fighting will be for the most part vain. If we cannot make possible to the American Indian the Four Freedoms that we say, and sincerely believe, are basic to the new world order, then they are impossible of achievement with any group anywhere.

We will freely grant that there are others among our citizens to whom this applies—the Negro, the American-born Japanese, and other racial and minority groups who in the main are denied the essentials of democracy; but we could well start by considering how these essentials of the American way of life can be secured to the American Indian.

He was our first and natural citizen. We owe it to the

Indian to give him a chance to be a full participant in our common life—economically, socially, politically, and religiously. While some real progress has been made during the past century, much still remains to be achieved, and there is not too much time left if the American Indian is to enter into these new freedoms at the close of the war. A study of the status of the American Indian at this time is thus most opportune.

Such a study demands of us that we think through the application of some of these principles that are basic to the new world order as we apply them to a significant minority group in our population. Again, it helps us to put into practice and to bring to fruition some of the reforms in our treatment of the American Indian that are long overdue. We may accomplish in the period of war what we could perhaps never achieve—certainly not in the same space of time—in a period of peace.

This book is an attempt to summarize changes in the status of the American Indian in the United States and—as far as limitations of space permit—in Canada. Its purpose is to portray in clear, simple language his history and cultural backgrounds, and to bring into focus the relations between Indians and whites, the economic and social conditions among Indian peoples, and the outstanding educational and religious developments of recent years; and, further, to reveal the present status of the Indian, and to suggest something of his place in the new world order.

These chapters all raise important and pressing questions that are involved in the present status of American Indians. It is highly desirable that the problem of wardship should be given special study at this time. In this moment in which democratic citizenship is being advocated on a world scale, it would seem to be the essence of consistency and good faith to release the Indian from wardship and make possible full participation in American life. Further economic, social, and educational progress appears to wait upon this important change in the Indian's status.

The first part of a report of a special Senate committee on Indian affairs is just off the press and contains suggestions of immediate sweeping changes, many of which are referred to in this volume. This adds to the timeliness of study and action on the wardship status of the American Indian.

There is another important aspect of this study that we do well to keep in mind. While we have stated that the Indians constitute one of the smallest of the minority groups in the United States, the approximately twenty-five million Indians in the Western Hemisphere represent a population factor that must be reckoned with in the days of reconstruction that are ahead. Whatever we do now to put the Indians of the United States on some sound foundation of democratic freedom will be of value as we think through and plan for the place of the Indians of other countries in the new world order.

A word needs to be said about the work of Christian missions among the Indians and the responsibility of the church in the issues with which this study is concerned.

The evangelical churches, both as denominations and in interdenominational enterprises, have carried on a commendable program, considering all the circumstances under which they have labored. But the time is now ripe for drastic readjustments. The suggested reforms that appear in these pages should be considered a primary responsibility of the mission boards. The recruiting, training, and use of native leadership in Indian missions are made more imperative by the changes that will follow the war. Native leadership is increasing but not with sufficient rapidity to meet the demands that are upon us and that will be even more imperative at the close of the war. The gradual merging of churches and institutions heretofore operated on a segregated level is another desirable goal.

The necessity of increasing the interdenominational work in Indian missions is made more urgent and acute by the war situation. We have too long confused the Indian by our denominationalism and should take advantage of the changing outlook to make possible a single Protestant impact.

Freedom from wardship, the absorption of Indian children and youth into the schools of the community, the assimilation of Indians wherever possible into the life of the community and especially into the churches of the community—these and many other forward movements call for the united support of the mission boards and the churches. The period before the ending of the war should be considered a prime opportunity to inaugurate some of these changes as part of progress leading to a more democratic order.

There is another important emphasis to be found in this volume—that of human consideration of the Indian. The time is long overdue for us to get away from the sentimental and the romantic and to think in terms of the realistic. The Indian is prepared or preparing to take his place in American life. He has already demonstrated his capacity to accept equal responsibility in all realms of professional, vocational, industrial, and business interests.

We therefore write this foreword in high hope and with every confidence that something worth while will attend the labors of all those who have given of their time and talent to the preparation of this book. A special word of commendation is due to Dr. G. E. E. Lindquist, the general editor and responsible author, who has labored without stint in the preparation of the volume. No person in the United States is better fitted by training and experience to assemble the material, and we would express thanks for this, another milestone advance in the progress of the study of the American Indian.

In closing we would express the hope that local churches and study groups may discover in this volume the basis upon which to institute some of the reforms that are uppermost in our thought on world affairs. However difficult it may be to achieve these things on a world scale among all the races, it would seem a reasonable suggestion that we might begin to apply them to the Indian in American life.

Chapter I

THE INDIAN IN AMERICAN LIFE

IN AN ISOLATED LOG CABIN OUT ON THE DAKOTA PRAIRIE, there hangs a service flag with two stars. Moses Slow Fly, a representative of the older generation, proudly points these out to the visitor and explains in his own language that one represents his son, who is a paratrooper, while the other star is for his daughter, who is a Wave. Mr. Slow Fly is making his contribution to the war effort not as an irreconcilable member of a conquered race but as an American citizen dedicated to the cause of freedom.

This rallying of the red man to the cause of democracy is highly significant. Today he is giving unstintingly to the prosecution of the war, not only in the vital defense industries but to the armed forces, in numbers greater in proportion than the white population—fully twenty thousand in the military camps and twice as many in war industries.

True, the American Indian has common cause with the Allies; he loves freedom and fully realizes that humanity needs the defense of the freedom-loving man. Furthermore, he is not harboring grievances because of the past. Not far from Mr. Slow Fly's humble abode is the government day school. Whether by chance or with a touch of irony, there hangs in its hall a large picture of Custer's last fight, a reminder of the bitter clashes between whites and Indians in the past century. He, as well as his neighbors, is willing to let bygones be bygones as far as relations of his ancestors with the early settlers and their government are concerned. In fact, he has gone forward to fight for some of the very freedoms denied him.

CONTRIBUTION TO THE WAR EFFORT

A recent study [1] of the mobilization of Indian manpower indicates that homes, schools, and reservations have been called upon not only to furnish these thousands for the armed forces, but also to supply non-draftable men and women to the essential war work of the nation. Consider what it means to our Indian citizens to have a General Tinker, the hero of Midway Island, and a Barney Old Coyote, twice decorated for valor, as members of their race. With a thrill they listen to radio accounts of the exploits of Company I, 180th Infantry, 45th Division, in the invasion of Sicily, and hear the names of Jimmie Holones of Fort Wingate, New Mexico, Corporal Moses Harjo of Chilocco, Sergeant Mack Tiger of Okemah, both from Oklahoma, and one New Yorker, Private Peter Lexanos, all exhibiting individual heroism on foreign shores.

Not only have Indian men and women distinguished themselves in all the services—as airmen and marines, as commissioned officers and privates, as scouts and interpreters, as Wacs and Waves—but industrial leaders and personnel experts have ascertained that the Indian has many skills and innate capacities that render him especially adaptable to the unusual requirements of a streamlined industry. Some who formerly referred to the Indian as lazy and lacking in ambition have found that his gifts of patience and interest in manipulative skills contribute toward making him a most valuable member

[1] All numbered references appear at the ends of chapters.

of the new industrial society. Then, too, it has been amply demonstrated that he responds favorably to work that challenges his interests and his loyalty to his country. The Indian is rapidly discovering that work, rather than any bountiful largess bestowed by Uncle Sam to satisfy "claims" for past hunting grounds, is going to be his salvation in today's as well as tomorrow's world.

Alex Whitefeather is an airplane mechanic who hails from a reservation in North Dakota. His wife is a Sioux. They have three lively youngsters. Alex has learned his trade so well that he has already received several promotions. Proudly he displays a highly commendatory letter from his superior. He is now stationed somewhere on Long Island, a far cry from his native Dakota prairies. Alex had come under Christian influence in a mission school, while Rose, his wife, had grown up in the Christian environment of a pioneer Sioux mission. What about their present church relations in this far-off land of skyscrapers and smoking chimneys? Rose would like to have her children attend Sunday school and desires appropriate prayers and Bible passages to teach them. Is there not a neighborhood church ready to receive these war workers in their midst? Yes, a local minister is notified, contacts are established, and presently both Alex and Rose are invited to the church night supper, while the children have found a Sunday school home.

Wichita, Kansas, is the center of extensive war industries. Because of its close proximity to old Indian territory as well as attractive offers for employment, hundreds of Indian youth, many of whom have been trained in welding and sheet-metal work at such schools as Haskell and Chilocco, have flocked to this and similar defense areas. The employment agencies have no data on Indian employees either as to number or location. It is, of course, significant to discover that no separate figures are readily available for Indians as there are for Negroes and even Jews. It would seem to indicate that there is practically no segregation and that Indians are accepted naturally and normally as indigenous elements of the population. Often, however, the housing situation is desperate. In common with other emergency workers, Indian youth find themselves crowded into the less desirable rooming houses and tenement districts. In the study already referred to, it was found that too often their recreational activities are limited to dancing in places where alcoholic beverages are provided, cheap movies, and slot machine gambling; that there is all too little home influence brought to bear upon these young people; that they are making little provision for future needs; that there is very little church attendance on the part of any appreciable number and very little follow-up by the churches of those who do attend. Here is a challenge to the Christian agencies of a defense industry area to devise ways and means of ministering to youth engaged under wartime conditions, a number of whom will never return to the deadening routine of reservation life.

At Hastings, Nebraska, another defense area, approximately 200 Indians (75 single men and 21 families) are employed in construction work. These represent a number of tribes, but the majority are fresh from the Dakota reservations. The single men are housed in barracks while the families are crowded into tents. When asked about their recreational life, they said: "There is nothing for us to do. We go up town and walk around the streets, go into a picture show or sit around in a tavern." As strangers in a strange land, not knowing the length of their habitation, few if any children find their way to school. In fact, the local school district is neither ready nor indeed too willing to accept these newcomers. Consequently, the children have a tendency to drif nd get into mischief. A welfare agency has helped a number f relief cases with food and clothing as well as by distribut- ng religious literature at Christmas and Easter. In common ith similar defense centers throughout the nation, the hurches are not prepared to cope with the sudden influx of roups with such varied racial and economic backgrounds. ome progress has been made, however, by the organization f an advisory committee under interdenominational auspices o render community service in which the Indian war workers vill be included.

Not only in industrial centers and war plants is the Indian aking his place in American life, but also on the farms, vhere he is learning the truth of the maxim: "Tickle the arth with a hoe, and she laughs with a harvest." Mr. Brings- hem-in-alive hails from a generation given over to the chase, s his name would indicate. But realizing that the hunting conomy was doomed with the passing of the buffalo and aving secured an allotment of agricultural land, he has set- led down, not without seasonal set-backs and recurrent mis- ivings, to the tilling of the soil. Today his country calls im, not to bear arms in Europe or the southern Pacific, but o increase his acreage, his herd, and his flocks in order to help eed the hungry and destitute. Without fanfare or thought f doing anything heroic, Mr. Brings-them-in-alive puts in his Victory garden, plows his fields, and cultivates his corn. And while some of his fellow-tribesmen make a hasty de- parture for the ever recurring powwows and rodeos, he quietly does the chores and cares for his cattle. When Sun- day morning comes, he serves as catechist or native helper at the near-by chapel. Once a month, however, he journeys with his family and neighbors to an improvised arbor on the creek bottom where he joins in the Day of Prayer services for the boys and girls serving the colors. This interesting and unique gathering calls together representatives from various denominations in the area, who take turns in leading the devotions raising their voices in song and prayer, earnestly petitioning the Almighty that peace may dawn on a warring world When evening falls, he hitches his team to the wagon for the journey back to the home and the duties awaiting him there

Who will question Mr. Brings-them-in-alive's right to a place in our American life? He is demonstrating his ability to assume that place and to hold it. May his number increase

Wooden Leg is the self-acclaimed chief priest of the medicine men of an isolated tribe in the Southwest. For years he has guarded the three sacred medicine bundles on which no white man has ever looked or ever is to look. He recognizes, however, the superior medicine of the white man and periodically makes his incantations to resist the overthrow of the ways of his ancestors. There is an epidemic of flu abroad in the land. This sickness has invaded his clan. Wooden Leg, being called, makes due preparations for a "sing" with all the paraphernalia involved. The evil spirits causing this disease must not go unsung. On arrival at the crude dwelling, he finds not only the patient, coughing and spitting, but his relatives well represented. In the crowded room, the ceremony proceeds: sing follows sing; incantation follows incantation. But the patient fails to recover. Within a given time, the relatives are victims of the dread scourge. Fortunately the visiting nurse and the agency physician, aware of the infectious epidemic, are able to institute alleviative measures before the disease has spread throughout the entire tribe. Wooden Leg escapes the ravages of the flu but his reputation as a medicine man suffers. Who will question the church's obligation to bring to Wooden Leg and his fellow-tribesmen the healing ministry of Christianity and its teaching so as to prepare them to become part of our composite national fe, to contribute their share to our Christian commonwealth, nd to join with us as citizens of the Kingdom to come?

'HE OLD HUNTING ECONOMY DOOMED

What happened to the red man when he was faced with vhat has been termed "Western acquisitive society" is re-orded in the history of the past four hundred and fifty 'ears, stirring years filled with stirring events. Territorial xpansion, involving new trade routes and new sources of evenue; the displacement of the fishing industry by the fur rade, with that trade penetrating the continent ever more leeply in search of new varieties of fur-bearing animals; the 'act that hunting Indians were soon left without food re-ources; the introduction of rum, powder, shot, and firearms, often used as gifts to curry favor; [2] the influence of monopoly ıssumed by the fur companies on Indian trade; the spread ›f epidemics, not necessarily due to European contacts, but probably augmented by them; and, last but not least, the ınvolvement of the New World in the wars among European states and the use of Indian fighters largely as pawns under the guise of "alliances"—these are some of the factors that inevitably led not only to what has been termed the "loss of a continent" but to what proved to be of far greater significance—the displacement of a way of life.

The hunting economy of the red man was doomed from the moment that prancing Arab chargers were taken off the Spanish caravels; from the moment that the crude cannon and muskets of Champlain sounded out across the waters of the lake that bears his name. It was a doom slow in progress, but as inevitable as the procession of day and night.

In the course of the white man's westward trek, the Indian, either through forced or voluntary removals, was often exposed to a cruel and relentless frontier. This is borne out by

the pointed remarks of James Barbour, then Secretary c
War, when he said in 1826, "They [the Indians] have bee
persuaded to abandon the chase to locate themselves an
become cultivators of the soil. . . . And when they hav
done so, you send your agent to tell them they must sur
render their country and recommit themselves to some nev
desert, and substitute as the means of their subsistence th
precarious chase for the certainty of cultivation." [3]

That our government to a greater degree than Canada an
the Latin American countries has pursued a course of oppor
tunism, with zig-zag policies pertaining to Indian affairs to
often in evidence, no one can seriously question. The agita
tion for western removal, the constant jostling about fron
pillar to post, the various attempts at concentration of Indian
in a territory beyond the Mississippi, all were inimical to th
assimilation of the native, the "incorporation of Indians int
white communities," as some termed it. Instead of solving th
so-called Indian problem by removals, the government lack
of policy perpetuated it. Thus, the anti-social influences of
tribalism, especially as instanced in its primitive divisivenes
and lack of cohesiveness, a carefully guarded and subsidized
segregation, as well as a resultant isolationism, have been pro-
longed throughout the period of Indian-white relations. And
the end is not yet.

INDIAN POPULATION PAST AND PRESENT

Just how many Indians inhabited the Western hemisphere
in the pre-Columbian era will probably never be known.
Students of the past have thus far furnished no reliable data.
In fact, some of the figures cited are quite fantastic. One
historian essays an estimate on the basis of the Indian population of the tidewater district of Virginia and that of California and arrives at the startling total of 3,000,000.[4] On the

ther hand, a somewhat conservative estimate is that offered n the following United States government report:

> From the best sources of information, it is doubtful whether he American Indians in what is now the United States exceeded he present number (346,962) at any time since the advent of Columbus, particularly if account be taken of the 60,000 or more who have surrendered their tribal identity and have mingled with he general population.[5]

Perhaps Dr. Clark Wissler, a leading American anthropologist, comes nearer the truth when he states that there never were very many Indians in this country, as compared with the present white population. He is inclined to disagree with those who estimate the number of Indians in the United States and Canada in 1780 as 1,000,000, and places the figure nearer 750,000.[6]

Though relatively few in number, if we except those of Central and South America, the Indians have awakened an interest well-nigh universal and have exerted an influence far beyond their numerical significance. A realization of this came to the writer on a lecture trip to Europe some years ago, where he found an amazing interest in all things Indian, especially Indian lore in all its manifestations. The children across the water "play Indian" just as our children do. Their imagination has been kindled not only by Pocahontas and the *Leatherstocking Tales*, but by Indian life on the prairie and the story of Sitting Bull. The Boy Scout movement, among others, has incorporated much of the spirit and atmosphere of the old Indian camp life into its organization. Then, too, Indian names have been given to our states and cities, rivers and lakes. These are, and will continue to be, constant reminders of their presence.

The Indian population of Canada[7] in 1852 was 124,578; in 1939 it was listed as 118,378. While this indicates a de-

crease over the decades, it nevertheless marks an increase o
1½ to 2 per cent per annum over that of recent enumera-
tions. In 1852 it was freely predicted that "in fifty years th
Indians will all be either dead or assimilated." Neither ha
happened.

There are 2,201 Indian reserves in Canada—of which 2,19
are listed as "occupied"—totaling 5,422,905 acres. The number of Indian agencies is 121, with seven inspectorates. Rather
interestingly the Indian Department in the Dominion comes
under the Bureau of Mines and Resources and the title given
to the head is that of Deputy Superintendent General of
Indian Affairs. His position, like that of our Commissioner
of Indian Affairs, is appointive.

Available government statistics give the Indian population of the United States and Alaska as approximately 400,-
000.[8] Obviously this includes people of varying degrees of
Indian blood whose names happen to be on tribal rolls as
well as those who through wardship, treaty, or inheritance
have acquired certain rights. This presence of the mixed-
blood as an increasingly dominant factor in Indian affairs is
an important element in all population data. Dr. H. L.
Shapiro in speaking recently of these mixed-bloods makes the
point that governmental paternalism has created "a sociologi-
cal and legal body of Indians whose blood is a mixture of the
Indian, white, and Negro elements in the population at large.
The census frankly admits this in its instructions to enumer-
ators, who are advised 'to return as Indians, not only those
of full Indian blood, but also those of mixed white and Indian
blood, except where the percentage of Indian blood is very
small or where the individual is regarded as a white person
in the community where he lives. . . .' This means that only
those with no detectable evidence of an Indian heritage may
escape the classification of Indian." [9]

What shall we say, then, to the oft-repeated dictum that the Indian is a vanishing race? The growth in population has been steady since about 1900. What is vanishing, in fact some would say has already vanished, is the full-blood Indian.

According to the census of 1935 at the Blackfoot Agency, Montana, out of a population of 4,300, only 934 were classed as full-bloods. The increase in population was recorded among the mixed-bloods, especially those of one-eighth and one-sixteenth degree; a decrease was noted among the full-bloods. From a study of the Pine Ridge Reservation, South Dakota, we glean the following:

The full-bloods are becoming fewer and the mixed-bloods are on the increase. In the figures available for 1930 to 1937 inclusive, the birth rates for all enrolled full-bloods vary from 19.5 to 37.6 (per 1,000 enrollees), while the birth rates for mixed-bloods vary from 27.4 to 44.6; the death rates for the full-bloods vary from 28.8 to 44.3, while that for the mixed-bloods varies from 8.0 to 13.4. In other words, the smaller death rate but larger birth rate among the mixed-bloods substantiates the inference drawn from the age-sex pyramids that the full-bloods are on the decrease while the mixed-bloods are on the increase.[10]

In 1934, at the fiftieth anniversary of the founding of Haskell Institute at Lawrence, Kansas, known far and wide as the government's largest Indian school, there were sixty-seven tribes represented in the student body. They came from twenty-five states. Of the 741 enrolled, only 204 were listed as full-bloods; the rest, of course, represented various degrees from seventh-eighths down. Truly the mingling of the races since the advent of the Norsemen, or shall we say Columbus, has left its indelible impress.

NOT A HOMOGENEOUS PEOPLE

While anthropologists seem fairly agreed that all Indians are essentially of one generalized racial type, it is well to recognize that they are not a homogeneous people.[11] With two hundred tribes or remnants of tribes, speaking many languages and dialects and scattered on at least one hundred and sixty different reservations in twenty-six states of the Union, one may readily understand that the Indian is in many respects as much of a composite as the Caucasian. No less an authority than Dr. M. W. Stirling, chief of the Bureau of American Ethnology, has reminded those who share the somewhat prevalent belief of a single, general Indian language that there are fifty-two linguistic stocks north of Mexico and approximately two hundred Indian languages that are mutually unintelligible. "Practically all of these have dialectic variations of sufficient degree to warrant recognizing them as dialects and the total of such dialects may be estimated at three times the above number of languages or six hundred."[12]

As the Indians roamed the great central plains season after season in quest of the bison, the need of a common means of communication developed into the use of a sign language.[13] With the passing of the buffalo, the need for this unique and picturesque sign language also languished. Today the Boy Scout organization has incorporated certain of the Indian signs into its rituals. Similarly in the coastal regions of Oregon and Washington, where numerous diverse dialects caused confusion in many villages, there grew up a jargon known as Chinook, by which these bands communicated with one another.

Although various attempts have been made in recent years to foster the use of native dialects, especially in the Southwest, through the introduction of phonetic methods of recording, English is increasingly the medium of expression. The children and young people, in common with their fellow-Americans of whatever racial background, express a preference for "the language of the land." On state occasions and when important tribal business is on the docket, often the most fluent English-speaking Indian may avail himself of an interpreter in order that all may share in the proceedings. In Pueblo council meetings, Spanish is often the medium of interpretation. Some of the larger tribes like the Sioux and, to a less extent, the Navajos, are bilingual. The early missionaries put these languages into writing, thus stimulating the translation of the Scriptures and the preparation of Christian literature in the Indian dialects; in the main, missionaries have encouraged bilingual expression.

SOME CURRENT MISCONCEPTIONS

After all the years of contact with these first Americans, it seems strange that fanciful notions about them are still held by many of their neighbors. One popular interpretation of the Indian has been given through the highly colored "Westerns" of the movies, which reflect not a distinctively Indian life but rather the cowboy culture to which the Indians were exposed as white settlement spread across the continent. Again, our pictures and fiction have often characterized the Indian youth as a modern Hiawatha who while off at school indulges principally in football, track, and hockey, and then when school days are over goes "back to the blanket" to "hibernate" on government rations and lease money.

Since the ubiquitous and thrill-hungry tourist has appeared on the American scene, certain commercial agencies that seek to exploit the spectacular have vied with one another in staging exhibitions of Indians in picturesque costumes, supposedly pre-Columbian, accompanied by tribal dances, some of which are said to show French ballet and Moorish influence. Needless to say, such shows give false impressions of dances that were originally ceremonial in their nature and largely connected with religious observances.

Canada has by no means escaped the stream of tourist traffic on Indian reserves, with attendant ceremonials of "adoption into the tribe" and the casual contacts of "intelligent tourists." George McDougall, "missionary, statesman, and hero," commenting in the 1870's on the significance of those trends, said: "One hardly knows how to apologize for the misstatements of intelligent tourists who travel these plains. Their descriptions of the 'noble, virtuous, honest Indians' are all from the ideal point of view. Let them come down to real work, study the language and lives of the people, live among them as your missionaries do, and then they will be able to appreciate the wonderful changes wrought by the gospel." [14]

Long before the highly romantic figure of the red man appeared from the pens of Chateaubriand and James Fenimore Cooper, there had been people on both sides of the Atlantic who had sought to confer such royal titles as "king," "emperor," and especially "princess" on the Indians. The historic example of this is, of course, "King Philip," the successor to Massasoit. And as for Indian princesses, their number has been legion. To this day there are those who masquerade under the title of princess, and to emphasize this "royalty" adorn their beaded headband with an eagle feather. Anyone cognizant of old Indian customs knows that such decorations were limited rather strictly to the members of the male sex, and then only for meritorious cause.

Such disrespectful labels as "lazy Indian," "good as a dead Indian," "can't be civilized any more than an Indian" are often used by the uninformed members of a dominant race to keep those of a minority group "in their rightful place." Someone has said that "every man is as lazy as he dares to be." The placing of practically an entire people on rations was the first experiment with the dole, unfortunately not the last. The paternalism thus fostered has laid the cold blight of dependency on the Indian people. It is expressed in the phrase often heard on the reservations, "Why work? Uncle Sam won't let us starve."

An Indian Service superintendent of many years' experience on the reservations is quoted in *A Wild Indian* as saying:

> The more I learn about Indians, the more convinced I am that their minds work the same way that ours do. I don't believe that they are lazier, as a class, more fatalistic, or more prodigal than we are, or would be in their circumstances. Yes, many Indians are shiftless, and so are many whites. Not one man in ten saves enough to support himself in his old age. The government assumes that we in the Civil Service are too improvident to save enough for our own old age, and acts as our guardian by taking a part of our salaries for a fund out of which to pension us at our retirement. Uncle Sam is not taking any chances on *our thrift*.[15]

The oft-repeated adage "no good Indian but a dead Indian" was coined in the old frontier days of cruel and relentless warfare and has no bearing on ethical qualities, past or present. As far as being "civilized" is concerned, much depends on what constitutes the end product, so to speak. From some aspects of our Western civilization, perhaps the Indian prays to be delivered.

On the other hand, there are those who assert that the Indian belongs to the Stone Age and that it is, and was, therefore, a mistake to try to civilize him. He is "a child of nature," they say; "civilization spoils him." Furthermore, "Don't educate him; that makes him common like the rest of us; let him live his own life in his own way." These romanticists who seek to maintain the *status quo* of pre-Columbian days seem to be indulging in a naïveté that closes their eyes to the blatant anachronism of their position, particularly when the Indians themselves do not desire to be different "for the sake of being different" nor to any perceptible degree resist the influences now making for social unity and harmonious cultural development. The educated Indian of today does not accept the false theory that, if a group possesses some peculiar cultural heritage or some treasure from the past, the thing to do is to withdraw from others in order to preserve it. Rather does he hold that the way to preserve any such treasure is to share it with his fellow-citizens of whatever racial background.

A PLEA AGAINST FALSE ROMANCE

Some idealizers of the past, under the high-sounding rallying cry of "religious freedom," not only tacitly encourage but seek by legislative enactment to revive and preserve the cult of the primitive.[16] Well does such a long-time student of Indian life and lore as Frances Densmore, formerly with the Bureau of American Ethnology, say in voicing a "plea against the false romance cloaking the American Indian":

> The present plea of romance is in behalf of the religion of the Indians. This is more subtle than the plea about his land and comes at a time when religious tolerance is in the air. We cannot return the land on which Chicago stands, and we find it rather diverting, on a summer vacation, to go watch the Indian worshipping the Great Spirit according to the dictates of his conscience. Every tourist, hotel keeper, and auto livery proprietor will defend this religious freedom of the red man. . . . The old religion of the Indian had its roots in the calm of meditation and a rigor of self-discipline which is foreign to the younger generation. . . . The true Indians

of the old type do not need legislation to enable them to keep their native religious concepts. Its essence will be inherited by those of their own race who are fitted to receive it and by the poets of all time. A student from a government school could not absorb this religion by receiving permission to "take part in a ceremony." [17]

That the Indian of an earlier day was a religious being, strong and steadfast in his adherence to ceremonial rites and usages, is a well attested fact. The very perils and hardships of the chase and warpath created in him a longing for some relationship with the unseen world of mystery round about him. So he established such relationships as he could through fastings and visions, sacrifices and immolations. The spirits that gave him good success in the chase and thus kept off starvation and famine were not to go unhonored or unsung. They became the *baalim* of the nomad's land, with the medicine men or priests as the chief exponents of this worship.

SUBJECTED TO MANY CHANGES

Anyone cognizant of the Indian peoples knows that they have been subjected to many changes, ill-advised experiments, and would-be reforms, governmental and otherwise. The Indian of the old trail, calm and meditative, moves slowly, although the life around him may be spinning in a veritable whirligig of change. Whenever a group of Indians are rushed into a new course of action or when something is "put over" on them in a hurry, they always suffer and often balk; there is invariably an unfavorable reaction. This is true of sudden legislative action, of abrupt and sudden shifts in their mode of living. Witness, for example, the promoting and building a decade or two ago of commodious frame houses among certain Apache bands in the Southwest to replace their crude wickiups. The casual traveler on a visit to the reservation finds a number of them boarded up and abandoned. On inquiry, he learns that a death has occurred and the "ghost fears" are at work. The house-building program was well intentioned but premature and did not take into consideration the superstitions still regnant among that particular people. Numerous other examples could be given, such as the transformation from the carefree camp life to the static conditions of reservation life, from buffalo hunting to agriculture, from a semi-nomadic existence to a more sedentary one.

However, in saying this, there is no thought of putting too much emphasis on the fancied injustice inherent in the Indian's having to conform to changing conditions and having to find his niche in present-day American life. Indian youth of today would be the first to resent such an allegation. The nation remembers the service of those enlisted in World War I. They were not segregated in separate units but mingled freely with their white comrades-in-arms. The same is true of the present conflict. Of course, some of them were dubbed "Chief So-and-So," all in a fine spirit of camaraderie. A Sioux war veteran, when asked how he got along, remarked, "Got along fine; first time in my life that I was taken for what I am, just another human being."

Let it be said as the closing thought of this chapter that our chief interest in the Indian is that he is a human being. The church of Christ owes him more because he is a human being than because he happens to be an Indian. Popular conceptions of "race," especially when they stress superiorities and differences, are often false and at times fraught with dangerous consequences. The Christian goal is to make all nations of the earth one. Its standards recognize no racial distinctions nor special privileged class or group. In the new Christian nature "there is no room for Greek and Jew, circumcised and uncircumcised, barbarian, Scythian, slave, or free man; Christ is everything and everywhere." [18]

The period from the primitive past to the highly complex life of the present covers a span of many centuries. In the next chapter, the cultural background of the American Indian is vividly presented according to the culture areas in which he moved, his comings and goings, his type of habitation and dress, his arts and crafts, his customs and ceremonies—highlights of the varied ways of living practised by the original inhabitants of this country.

"But didn't we take his land from him, and hasn't he been subjected to drastic changes ever since Columbus discovered America?" are among the frequent questions addressed to workers among Indians. A brief summary of the history of Indian-white relations from colonial times to the present is found in Chapter Three with special emphasis on policies, past and present, that led to the development of wardship. There follows in Chapter Four a discussion of economic, health, and social adjustments that have formed an integral part of this transition period. The influence of what Indians used to call "the white man's black on white" (books) and his "go-see-writing" (schools), all that we are accustomed to include when we speak of education, comes in for consideration under Chapter Five.

That which gives meaning and purpose to missionary literature is the story of new life on new trails, the Christian contribution to Indian life, discussed in Chapter Six. And the importance of this study of the Indian in American life is further enhanced by devoting the closing chapter to his part in the post-war world and to the church's task and the new day.

REFERENCES

1. Presented by A. Willard Jones of Chilocco, Oklahoma, at the Oklahoma Regional Fellowship Conference, Bacone College, June, 1943.

2. "It is hardly an exaggeration to say that the fur traders who swarmed into the Northwest between 1768 and 1783, the date when the Northwest Company was organized, deluged the Indian country with alcohol." *Beaver, Kings and Cabins*, by Constance L. Skinner, p. 236. New York, The Macmillan Co., 1933.
3. Report to House Committee on Indian Affairs and quoted in *A Continent Lost—A Civilization Won*, by Jay P. Kinney, p. 59. Baltimore, Johns Hopkins, 1937.
4. *American Indian Frontier*, by W. C. Macleod, p. 16. New York, Alfred A. Knopf, 1928.
5. Interior Department News-Release of October 6, 1924, as quoted in the New York *Times*.
6. Clark Wissler, Curator in Chief of Anthropology at the American Museum of Natural History, New York, in *Natural History*, quoted in *The Literary Digest*, September 15, 1934, p. 17.
7. *The Coming of the White Man*, by H. J. Priestly, p. 89. New York, The Macmillan Co., 1930.
8. According to the statistical supplement to the annual report of the Commissioner of Indian Affairs for the fiscal year ended June 30, 1940, the "Indian population under Indian Affairs January 1, 1940, totals 394,280."
9. *The Changing Indian*, edited by Oliver La Farge, chapter on "The Mixed Blood Indian," by H. L. Shapiro, p. 20. Norman, University of Oklahoma Press, 1942.
10. "An Economic and Social Reconnaissance Survey of the Pine Ridge Indian Reservation," by Allan G. Harper, U. S. Department of Agriculture, TC-BIC-1939.
11. An historian contributes the following: "The most striking facts with regard to the American Indian are his physical uniformity and his cultural diversity." From *Basis of American History*, by Livingston Farrand, p. 262. New York, Harper & Brothers, 1904.
12. Letter to author of June 25, 1943.
13. In the Smithsonian Institution, Washington, D. C., there is a sound film on the sign language, prepared by the late Major General Hugh L. Scott, a very valuable recording of an Indian art now fast disappearing. It is to be noted that the sign language was also shared by the Indians of the Canadian North-

west, more especially by members of the Blood, Blackfeet, Sarcee, and Stony (Sioux) tribes.

4. *One Hundred Years of Canadian Methodist Missions*, by Mrs. Frederick C. Stephenson, p. 104. Toronto, The Young People's Forward Movement, 1925.
5. *A Wild Indian*, by G. F. Miller, p. 459. Washington, The Daylion Co., 1942.
6. See S. 2755 Title II, Sec. 2, p. 24, 73rd Congress, 2nd Session; also Circular No. 2970, January 3, 1934, issued by the Commissioner of Indian Affairs.
7. "Plea against the False Romance Cloaking the American Indian," by Frances Densmore, in *The Christian Science Monitor*, July 25, 1928.
8. *Colossians* 3:11. From *The Bible: A New Translation*, by James Moffatt. Harper & Brothers, publishers.

Chapter II

CULTURAL BACKGROUNDS

by Erna Gunther

FOURTEEN NINETY-TWO! THAT IS THE ACCEPTED DATE for the discovery of America—but we generally fail to add, from the Atlantic; for centuries earlier America was discovered and colonized from the Pacific. Probably ten thousand years ago some fishermen—yearning even then for the catch in the next stream—crossed Bering Strait and, finding familiar-looking country, continued their fishing, unaware that they were on another continent. Columbus did not fully realize his momentous discovery, nor did these Stone Age fishermen who first came across the Strait dream that they were standing on the threshold of two continents.

Who were these fishermen from Asia? They belonged to the Mongoloid race and through centuries had been wandering northward. For many centuries more they streamed into America, gradually populating the two continents. As they settled in isolated places and intermarried in small groups they developed the specific physical types of the American Indian, and that development differentiated them more and more from their Asiatic origins. This theory of migration is speculative, but it is based on scientific evidence that points toward these conclusions. One of the great tasks of American anthropologists is to find the facts necessary to fill in this framework of speculation, and progress toward this goal is slowly being made by the archeologists who work eagerly every year during the short digging season afforded them by the brief Arctic summer. All the evidence fits into the framework already set up, and perhaps some day we can expect more substantial data on which to found our suppositions.

To describe the Indian in a more detailed fashion, we find everywhere he has straight black hair, dark eyes, fairly high cheek bones, a skin that ranges from yellow to reddish brown, and considerable variation in stature. In early literature he was given the name "red man," but actually there are very few Indians that can be called red. In the central part of North America there are a few tribes with a reddish tinge to their skins, but they are largely outnumbered by those who are much more yellow or brown in skin color.

In Europe the tallest people are found in the northern part of the continent, regardless of their nationality; a mixed group occupies a broad band in the central part; and the shortest people live in the south along the Mediterranean. In America these bands also exist, but they would run vertically, if spotted on a map, instead of horizontally. The tallest Indians are in the central part of North America; they shade off to slightly shorter people on the Atlantic seaboard; but on the Pacific coast, the population takes a decided drop in stature. Just as in Europe the difference in stature is not reflected in their achievements, so in America the short people on the Pacific coast developed many remarkable features of culture.

CULTURE AREAS

In Europe we compare nationalities as to customs, government, and language. In Indian America, there were also such differences, but they were not recognized clearly until the early settlers had traveled far enough into the country and seen Indians who differed substantially from those whom they had met on the Atlantic seaboard. Even then, to people who were trying to settle an unknown wilderness, the Indians were an obstacle, not groups whose interesting customs anyone wanted to study. One tribe seemed to scalp as well as another. Years of waiting intervened before these differences were scientifically described. When the anthropologists began to analyze Indian culture, they found it convenient to divide the country into culture areas. Dr. Wissler in his book *The American Indian* popularized the term and while there are many weaknesses in this classification, it simplifies study. Each area consists of tribes that share certain customs, both in ways of living and in social and ceremonial life. While most culture areas are by no means completely homogeneous, there is a general similarity that binds the group together.

When the first wanderers came into America from Asia, they had nothing but an untouched continent before them. If these first immigrants to America went along the valley of the Yukon and into the interior of the continent, they probably encountered rigorous weather, but no worse than they had known; if they went along the interminable, broken shore line, they battled fogs and tides, but usually had enough to eat. Since these early migrations are still a matter of speculation, it may prove profitable to turn to some of the explorers known to history and review what they found as they penetrated the continent from various directions.

THE SOUTHEASTERN TRIBES

In the four hundred and fifty years since the New World was discovered, the Indians have undergone many drastic changes. Had Columbus actually come to the mainland of

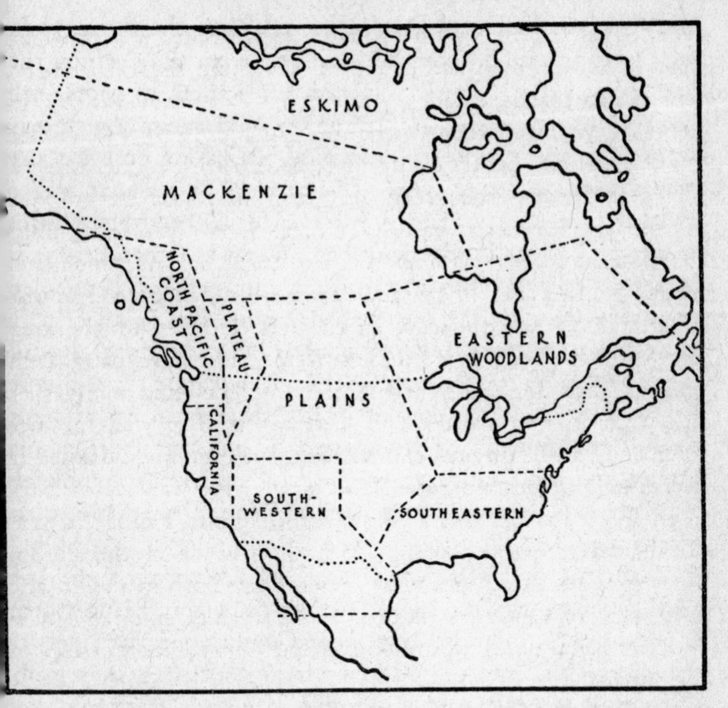

INDIAN CULTURE AREAS IN NORTH AMERICA

Adapted from *The American Indian: An Introduction to the Anthropology of the New World*, by Clark Wissler (see page 45).

North America he would probably have landed among tribal groups now known as Seminoles, of whom several hundred still live in the Everglades, while others have moved to Oklahoma. They, together with the Yuchi, Creek, Cherokee, Chickasaw, and others occupying the territory as far north as Virginia, formed the group now designated by anthropologists as the Southeastern culture area. Some lived in swampy shorelands and others on good agricultural land of which they made effective use. They raised maize (Indian corn), pumpkins, melons, and tobacco. In the western part of the area, they hunted deer, bear, and buffalo. Fish were caught by poison—as is done in South America today—and many shell fish were used on the coast. The tribes lived in well fortified towns and made dugout canoes for traveling. They dressed in deerskins and buffalo robes, and wove some fabrics of bark fiber. They made baskets of cane and splints, similar in material, technique, and design to baskets made in the Philippines. Good pottery was made, resembling both in design and shape that of Central America. There were ceremonial houses and temple squares where fires were burned in worship of the sun.[1]

In most parts of America, Indian society was democratic; the Southeast was one of the exceptions. The chief was regarded as a descendant of the Sun God and under his sacred influence, and below him there were four classes of people. A political system of strong confederacies was developed and the tribe was really a functioning unit. This stands in contrast to the weak tribal organization west of the Rocky Mountains. It is even difficult to define the tribal organization there. On the ceremonial side these people had elaborate planting and harvest rituals, a trait found among many agricultural people. At their "busk" festival the new fire was kindled, and the people purified themselves by use of the "black drink."

During the seventeenth and eighteenth centuries, this tribal life was broken up and many groups were realigned. Considering this break with the past, it is amazing that so much of the former customs of these tribes have actually been recorded, a service for which one must thank patient anthropologists like Dr. Frank Speck and Dr. John Swanton.[2]

THE EASTERN WOODLANDS AREA

Moving northward from the Southeastern culture area one comes to the Eastern Woodlands, a vast territory with many variations in customs and physical character. This stretches westward to Lake Superior and northward to the Arctic, where its people meet the Eskimo. This culture area, like the Plains and the Northwest Coast, extends into Canada and the aboriginal customs of the Indians did not change at any present international boundary. The people of the Eastern Woodlands were immortalized by James Fenimore Cooper, and, since his works were translated into many European languages, are the only Indians known to many Europeans. The Southern Algonquin and Iroquois were also agricultural, raising the same products as the Southeastern people. It was from these tribes that the Pilgrims learned how to plant corn and roast it, that turkeys were good to eat, and to turn an Indian harvest festival into our Thanksgiving. They also taught the whites to make journeycake and to have clambakes.

They supplemented their farming products with hunting, fishing, and gathering wild fruits. Around the Great Lakes, wild rice flourished and still does today. It provided a fine food crop. The western tribes hunted buffalo, while those in the east contented themselves with deer. The northern tribes shared the caribou hunt with the Eskimo.

Just as food habits varied, so did housing. People like the

Ojibway, Cree, and Salteaux lived in conical skin- or bark-covered shelters, while the tribes on the Atlantic seaboard lived in similar shelters in the winter, but moved into rectangular bark-covered houses in the summer. Clothing throughout the region was very much alike, the materials and quantity conforming to the local conditions. Leggings, breech clout, sleeved shirts, and soft-soled moccasins were worn by the men; and a skirt and jacket, or a one-piece dress, was the characteristic costume of the women. A fabric of bark fiber was woven with the fingers. Bark was also used for household utensils. Stone tools were universal, but in prehistoric times much copper was used by the people in the central region.

The birchbark canoe, associated in the popular mind with all Indians, was used by the tribes in the northern part of this area, while those in the south used the dugout similar to that used in the Southeast. For winter travel the northern peoples used snowshoes and toboggans.

In social and political life the real distinction between the Algonquin tribes and the Iroquois comes out. The Algonquin generally had a simple family organization with independent villages, but the Iroquois developed a system of descent through the mother, who was not only the head of her family but also represented it politically. This descent reckoned through the mother is referred to as a clan organization, and is found among many primitive groups. Among the Iroquois, it was exceptionally well developed, for the clan formed not only the basis of the family but also the nucleus of a system of representative government unparalleled in Indian America. The tribes were further bound together into the "League of Six Nations," with a government that carried on some systematic conquests.

The decorative art of this area was largely executed within

the historic period with materials secured from trade with Europeans. The French brought in the technique of ribbon-work, which is now being revived in Oklahoma. The traders brought beads, which replaced the porcupine quill embroidery, formerly done on buckskin. Beaded designs were worked in floral patterns and resembled the designs etched in the birchbark kettles. Their basketry was largely utilitarian and not an outstanding art like that of many other tribes; the same was true of their pottery. An art form linked with ceremonialism was the mask used in the rituals of the secret societies.

Ceremonial life of these people included the celebration of a corn festival, secret-society dances, and, in the western part of the area, the great Midiwiwin or Medicine Lodge ceremonies. There they also shared with tribes of the Plains culture area the use of ceremonial bundles for war and hunting, and a fixed ritual for procedure in conducting a war party. The individual also went out on the guardian spirit quest, as was regularly done to the westward.

As in the Southeast, the aboriginal culture of these tribes is difficult to reconstruct, since they have been in contact with whites from the earliest appearance of the French, Dutch, and English. But once more the painstaking work of a few anthropologists has brought this culture together into a fairly integrated picture. Today there are very few Indians left along the Atlantic coast, but near Buffalo there are a number of Iroquois, and many of the western tribes of this area are still to be found fairly near their historic locations.

PLAINS CULTURE TRAITS

Since the westernmost tribes of the Eastern Woodlands exhibit so many Plains culture traits, it is most logical to proceed to that area. Extending from the Mississippi to the

Rocky Mountains and practically from the Gulf of Mexic
to the tundra of Canada, they, like the Woodlands people
are well known historically. White persons who were no
brought up on James Fenimore Cooper but who read th
more recent "Westerns" are familiar with Indians who rod
horses, lived in circles of tepees, wore gorgeous feathered wa
bonnets, shot buffalo, and lay in wait for the unwary traveler across the great plains. The physical type of this Indian
has been used in the coinage of the United States on both th
nickel and the penny.

Few people stop to think that the horse, which they regard
as practically one with the Indian, was a relatively new
acquisition to which the Plains Indians themselves had just
become adjusted before the white explorers began to come
into their country.[3] The horse brought so many changes into
Plains culture that in discussing the history of the area the
distinction between conditions before and after the coming
of the horse needs to be noted.

Before the Plains peoples secured horses to facilitate travel,
the tribes—especially those in the Dakotas, Nebraska, and
Iowa—lived in villages of earth. They planted corn, and in
the summer, when their crops were well started, they went
out on foot for the communal buffalo hunt, under recognized
leaders who planned the trip and directed the hunt itself.
During this expedition they lived in small skin-covered tepees. Their kill was butchered and the meat dried so that
larger quantities could be carried home. After the hunt they
returned home and harvested their corn, which had flourished
or not according to the kindness of the elements.

The horse was introduced from the Southwest, where it
had been brought by the Spaniards as they pushed north
after the conquest of Mexico. Its use gradually spread north-
eastward as one tribe traded with another. Then it was traded

westward, until by 1750 it was a familiar sight in almost every Indian camp between the Mississippi and the Rocky Mountains. As the many tribes became accustomed to this important cultural innovation, their ways of life were changed, not so much through the introduction of new traits, however, as through the accentuating of trends already established. Instead of planting corn and then going on the buffalo hunt, they went hunting for a longer season and gradually abandoned the planting altogether. Instead of living in earth lodges in the winter, they made larger, sturdier tepees and lived in them all year. It was the woman's job to dress the skins for the tepee, sew them together, set up the tepee and take it down, and keep the skins in repair. This sounds like a great deal of work and there is no denying that it was, but Plains women developed an efficiency that was remarkable. Even today, when tepees are not used very much, contests in erecting them and taking them down are often features at Indian gatherings. Also, after the coming of the horse, the Plains tribes gave up making pottery, because it is just as difficult to carry it on continuous camping trips as is our chinaware. For cooking they used a skin container, as well as earth ovens, and followed the usual camping expedient of roasting meat by an open fire.

One of the interesting features of Plains Indian culture is the perfect adaptation of the objects they made and used to their manner of life. All their possessions folded and packed easily; they were not breakable. One of their principal forms of decoration on clothing and horse trappings was fringe. Have you ever seen Plains Indians today in a parade with all the fringe on their clothing and saddle bags moving gently as they ride along? It is a mode of decoration that looks best in motion, and of all people in North America they were most frequently on the move.

After the widespread use of horses had made them a no madic people, they did not wander at random, but at th same season each year could be found in approximately th same area, primarily because some favorite food was availabl there, some roots or berries, buffalo or elk or antelope herds Tribes who wander instead of remaining in permanent set tlements are often regarded as shiftless and as living with a unplanned economy. With the Plains people that is not true It took great foresight to be at the right place for huntin and for gathering a wild crop when it was ripe. It took care-ful planning to move families with all their possessions ir reasonable comfort over an area where extremes of tempera-ture are encountered both in winter and in summer. Th test of any mode of life is the degree of adaptation to environ-ment that it insures for the people who follow it and thei consequent prosperity and happiness. It seems to anthropolo-gists who have studied the Plains tribes that they achieved these ends.

THE PLATEAU CULTURE

Between the Rocky Mountains and the Coast range there is a semi-arid region known as the Plateau of Western Amer-ica. It does not have much to recommend it climatically; it is high land, largely in the drainage basin of the great Co-lumbia River, and north and west of that including the upper waters of the Fraser. When the early fur traders first encountered the people of this region, they had just devel-oped closer contact with the Plains tribes through the use of the horses secured in trade. With better transportation, the Plateau tribes, such as the Flathead and Kutenai, quickly adjusted themselves to a Plains way of living and went on longer and more extensive buffalo hunts. Gradually the use of the horse and some of the traits and customs of Plains ndians extended farther west to reach the Nez Percé and he Yakima and to other Sahaptin-speaking people farther outh. The ease of movement with the horse, the wild hrill of the buffalo hunt, the joy of making more elaborate uckskin clothing, and for the young men the excitement of he Plains pattern of war brought about a quick change in he whole aspect of Plateau culture. In contrast, the Salish-peaking people—now living on the Colville Reservation—ike the Sanpoil and Nespelem, retained their slower way of iving, using horses, doing a little more hunting, but not dopting the Plains social attitudes. In this century there as been found in eastern Washington the curious aspect of wo cultures that form a historical continuity existing side by side.

EXTENSION OF THE PLATEAU CULTURE

In the north, the Plateau culture merges with that of the great Mackenzie basin and is represented by the Northern Athapascan tribes like the Carrier, Chilcotin, Sekani, Dogrib, and, turning westward into the Yukon valley, the Kutchin and Tanana. Southward, the Plateau culture shades into the Great Basin with its Shoshonean tribes, who, like the eastern Plateau people, have taken on many Plains traits. The "Snake" Indians were Shoshoneans who were feared by the early travelers in this region as well as by their more peaceful neighbors. The Great Basin includes many diverse groups ranging from these Plains-like ones in the northeast to the seed-gathering tribes on the eastern slopes of the Sierra Nevadas. Like the Plateau, the area is bound together to a great extent by the fact that many of these tribes lack some of the spectacular customs of their neighbors.

In the southern part of the Great Basin are the warlike Ute, who worried the quiet farmers of the Southwest just as the Snake preyed on their neighbors. In this region the political organization so well established in the East and still holding strong in the Middle West disappears and the definition both of the chief and the tribal unit is uncertain. People lived in small bands, partly for an economic reason. Their territory did not produce enough food for large groups. They moved about because the search for food had to be conducted over a large terrain. Their household possessions were few and light, baskets being used for almost everything, a trait that ties them to the California area.

THE SOUTHWEST CULTURE AREA

Bordering on the Great Basin in the south are New Mexico and Arizona, which comprise the Southwest culture area famous for its Navajo, Apache, and Pueblo tribes. Their art and ceremonials are as well known to white Americans interested in Indian life as the horse-riding Indian is to the habitués of Western movies. The Gallup ceremonials combine many of the famous dances of the Southwest, even though not done there in their aboriginal settings. This area has a long history, which the archeologists have traced back through many centuries before the Spanish invaders came from Mexico.

In myth these people trace their wanderings from the place where they emerged from a hole in the earth's surface, after living far underground in very unpleasant surroundings. In their journey southward they looked for the center of the world, where they wanted to build their pueblos. The journey took many generations and on the way they learned all the arts of life, like planting crops, crafts, and ceremonials. On part of the journey they were entertained by the dancing gods, the Kachinas, but once an unthinking individual made fun of their grotesque faces and figures, so the

Kachinas told the people that they were offended and would no longer stay with them. They retired to the lake of the gods, but before they left they allowed the people to copy their costumes in order that man might imitate them in his dances. That is the origin of the Kachina dances, which can still be seen today; the Pueblo people divide their year into two halves, when the gods are with them, and when they are away. The change comes at the winter and summer solstice. The combination of mythology and archeology gives the Southwest a feeling of antiquity not encountered elsewhere in Indian culture in the United States.

For some time in the past the peoples of the Southwest area have been divided according to mode of life into three groups: the Pueblos, the camp-dwellers, and the village people along the Colorado River.

The Pueblos

Among the well known Pueblo tribes are the Zuñi, Hopi, Acoma, Taos, Laguna, Santo Domingo, Santa Clara, and the dwellers in many other small pueblos along the Upper Rio Grande. The most stationary of the Southwest groups, they have aptly been called by Dr. Ruth Underhill the "Penthouse Dwellers."[4] They live in great apartment houses built of masonry and adobe, each consisting of many rooms and sheltering a number of families. Many pueblos were built on high mesas for protection against Navajo and Ute marauders. Often a single trail up the mesa was the only one that needed to be defended, as at Acoma.

These Pueblo people were farmers, but strangely enough they did not live on their farms. They combined in a peculiar way the traits of both farming and town living. Surrounding each pueblo at a distance of up to seven miles lay attached farming villages. Here each family had a rude hut where they stayed overnight at those seasons when the crops needed special attention. Otherwise they went out early in the morning, cultivated their fields, and returned home for breakfast. Their crops were similar to those of the Southeast—corn, squash, melons, beans. Corn was ground on the *metate* to varying degrees of fineness and used as a basic food in the form of bread and corn cakes, as well as a thickening for rabbit and venison stews. The men contributed to the larder through hunting deer and antelope, and communal rabbit hunts provided fine meals and picnics for the whole group.

Along with the *metate* for grinding corn, every household had a number of cooking pots and water jars. Serving a humble purpose in their original setting, they are beautiful enough to be placed in both anthropological and art museums. The pottery of the Pueblos is one of the outstanding Indian crafts in America. It is still being made and it points an unerring finger at the past of its makers. Throughout the area, the archeologist dates his finds by the style and character of the broken pottery he encounters. Each group developed distinctive styles in historical succession. The pots were made from clay locally mined and shaped by the coiling method. Their remarkable symmetry pays a high tribute to the skill of the women who made them. After the pot had dried, it was painted and then fired in a crude oven. It takes a remarkably short time to make a pot, but every movement has to be exact and sure. Free-hand painting of beautiful geometric or semi-realistic designs was sometimes done by men as well as by women. The designs included the terraced clouds, lightning, rain, the germinating corn and sprouting bean, all symbols of their ceremonial interest in the rain on which they were dependent for their crops. In fact, the agriculture of this region is carried on in spite of unfavorable climate. The small amount of rainfall is essential to the last

rop. If this rain should fail, the Pueblos would starve. The
nportance of rain is stressed in their ceremonial life, and
ne gods are closely connected with rain, fertility, and crops.
esigns symbolizing these concepts appear on the pottery and
ccur frequently in Pueblo art. One interesting pottery dish
sed to contain cornmeal for ceremonial purposes even has a
mbolic shape. It is square, with sides terraced or step-like
long the top, representing the clouds, the symbol of rain.

he Camp-Dwellers

As we turn to the Navajos we come to the second large
ubdivision of the Southwest. The camp-dwellers were
ormerly nomadic hunters and gatherers, but after the Span-
ard introduced horses, sheep, and cattle, they became herds-
nen. Their material life was much simpler than that of the
Pueblos, but their ceremonial life was very complex. They
ived in earth-covered houses, called *hogans,* planted a little
orn, but much preferred to raid a pueblo with full storage
ooms after the harvest. They made a little very crude pot-
ery. They borrowed many customs from the Pueblos, in-
luding weaving. Before Spanish days, the Pueblo people
rew cotton for their weaving, which was gradually replaced
by wool after sheep had become common. The Navajo be-
ame skilled weavers and for several centuries have produced
he blankets for which they are famous. While Pueblo weav-
ng is done by men, the work among the Navajos is done by
women. Amsden, in his book on Navajo weaving, traces the
history of design and shows the development of the Navajo
blanket through successive periods of native yarn and commercial wools, vegetable dyes and aniline dyes. These blankets were originally worn as part of the costume and were
also used as bedding.

Much in Navajo ceremonial life was also borrowed from

the Pueblos. As was noted in the discussion of Pueblo pot tery, the dominant concept in ceremonial was prayer fo rain. The Navajo, in borrowing these ceremonies, retaine much of the form, but their purpose was changed to that o curing the sick. Both peoples seemed satisfied with the result they achieved. The corn dance of the Zuñi honored the cor goddess, the snake dance of the Hopi was a direct prayer fo rain. The use of snakes was not just a spectacular piece o bravado, but grew out of the belief that snakes were th messengers of the gods. During the dance a prayer for rain i breathed onto them and then they are released on the edge o the mesa and sent to the gods with it. Interesting to note i how the economy and the religion of these people were inter twined, for then one can realize how the destruction of on of these features would necessarily affect the other. That of course, is true of the customs of any society. All cultur traits are interdependent and to destroy any one trait harm the whole structure, just as an injury to any part of a livin organism affects the entire being.

The great ceremonials of the Navajo were the Mountai Chant and the Night Chant, both rituals conducted for th curing of the sick. The mythological background and th masked figures that appeared in these dances were part of th ceremonial complex shared with the Pueblos.

Living along the northeastern, eastern, and southern borders of New Mexico and Arizona were the Apache, with bands such as the Jicarilla sharing many culture traits with their Plains neighbors like the Kiowa. The Apache in southern Arizona, on the other hand, were more like the Pima and Papago. The Apache were nomadic, lived in lightly buil brush shelters, and, until herds were introduced, subsisted largely by hunting. They made no pottery, but did weave strong, durable, and handsome baskets. They, like the Navajo, were representatives of the great Athapascan-speaking language family, which is spread over America from the valley of the Yukon to northern Mexico.

Village-Dwellers along the Colorado

This leaves in the Southwest culture area only the Indians who lived along the Colorado and Gila Rivers in small villages or *rancherías,* as they were commonly called. Among them were the Yuma, Havasupai, Walapai, Maricopa, Yavapai, and Mohave, and the Pima and Papago on the Mexican border of Arizona. All were agricultural, the intensity of this activity depending on their immediate environment. They also gathered such fruits and seeds as the desert around them yielded, and, as with the Havasupai, spent half the year hunting. Crafts in this region were not done with the fine technique of the Pueblos; the same indifference also applied to their social life. In spite of the apparent lack of internal cohesion, however, there was a sense of tribal unity that centered around two interests—the tribal chief and the conduct of war.

The tribal chief of the Yuma, for example, had to have visionary power through which he could guide his people and promote their welfare. Every act of his depended upon an auspicious dream. In battle he had to remain apart, for the integrity and strength of the tribe depended on the security of his person. In contrast to the peaceful Pueblos, these Lower Colorado tribes were engaged in small warfare all the time. Food gathering and agriculture took relatively little of their time, and they had no elaborate ceremonials; so they gained their morale from war. A formalized ritual battle is still one of the features of the annual ceremony where the dead are mourned and the well-being of the living increased.

THE CALIFORNIA CULTURE AREA

Nearest neighbors of these Lower Colorado River tribes in California were people like the Diegueño and Luiseño who resembled them closely. On the coast of California, well northward to San Francisco, the Indians lost their native culture very early during the Spanish rule. They clustered around the missions and even became known by the mission name—as, for instance, the "San Gabrieleno"—thus losing all their tribal identity. Under these conditions modern anthropologists have been able to learn very little about them. North of San Francisco the Indians fared better, tribally speaking, and still consist of fair-sized groups that have been carefully studied. Their mode of life was typically Californian, hunting deer, gathering seeds, wild fruits, and berries. Their household utensils were mostly of basketry and in this craft they were probably the world's finest workmen. Among them the names of the Pomo, Miwok, and Washo are outstanding. Farther north along the lower Klamath, the Trinity, and the Humboldt Rivers, were the Hupa, Karok, and Yurok tribes, who shared many of their customs with the Northwest coast tribes but like their fellow-Californians had beautiful baskets for every use, from hats to salmon plates.

Even this brief survey shows how the culture area we call California is subdivided. In the southern part the relationship to the Southwest is pronounced; in the center there is the most distinctive culture; to the north, the customs resemble those of the tribes of Washington and northward.

THE NORTHWEST PACIFIC COAST

Perhaps the least known of the important culture areas of America is the Northwest Pacific Coast. While occasional Spanish ships visited this coast during the days of Spanish rule n California, this region did not attract much attention from he English-speaking world until Captain Cook made his eport on it after his voyages during and immediately follow-ng the American Revolution. In 1792 another Englishman, Captain Vancouver, sailed along these coasts and settled the dispute over this territory with the Spaniards, traded with the Indians, and saw the possibilities of the fur trade. Meanwhile, much farther north in Alaska, the Russians had secured a toe-hold and were exploiting the wealth in furs that that territory yielded. This glance at history will show how recently this part of Indian America became known to the white man in comparison with the areas touched by the Spanish invasion of the Southwest in the sixteenth century and by the settlement of the Atlantic coast in the seventeenth. When this vast region was opened up to the whites, they came in so fast and exploited the country for their own ends so thoroughly that even though little more than a century has passed, the Indian cultures of the Northwest have suffered more disruption than, for instance, the Pueblos with their centuries of contact with foreign peoples.

This area consists of the strip of land west of the Cascade Mountains and stretching from the southern border of Oregon to southeastern Alaska. The international boundary did not exist in this culture, and without the link of British Columbia the relationship between the Indians of Washington and those of Alaska would be difficult to understand.

Along this broken shore line Indians lived in small villages, often closely spaced. Had this situation prevailed in the Eastern Woodlands instead of the Northwest there would have been some political relationship among these villages; but here not only was that lacking, but there was no obvious organization within the village itself. In these communities each person had a definite social position, which was determined by his wealth and the prestige of his immediate ancestors. The people were divided into an upper class including the wealthy men and their relatives, and a lower class of common or poor people. There were also the slaves, unfortunate captives taken in raids and held as chattels. The status of the slave class was fixed; that of the other two was changing and uncertain. If a person lost his social prestige through failure to return his *potlatch* gifts or fulfill the obligations of his family, he would gradually slip from the upper class into the lower group. If a poor man had exceptional luck and succeeded in accumulating enough surplus goods to give a big *potlatch* and thus raise his status, his family might eventually be counted among the upper class. These changes were gradual and furnished good meat for the village gossips.

Potlatches and slave raids, major aspects of tribal life in the Northwest, demand careful examination.

The *potlatch* was a large feast provided by a man, with the help of his family, to which he would invite all the important people from the neighboring villages and tribes. After several days of feasting, dancing, and other amusements, the climax came when the host gave away to chosen guests large amounts of property in the form of canoes, slaves, blankets, food, and materials of all kinds. Of course after foreign traders reached these Indians, the character of these gifts changed greatly. Each person who accepted such a gift obligated himself to return another gift to the host, greater in value than the one he received. Among some tribes, such as the Kwakiutl of northern Vancouver Island, the increase in value of the gift returned was generally about one hundred per cent. This return had to be made in a reasonable amount of time, at least in a few years. Through this gift-giving the host gained in respect and standing among the tribes from which his guests came, and his family reflected his glory.

Important men gave only a few *potlatches* in a lifetime, so great was the task and expense of preparing for them. Each feast put the family higher on the social ladder. From the economic angle these feasts were also interesting, for they were the basis on which was founded the most capitalistic society in Indian America. The *potlatch* was really a fine investment system, with a rate of interest never dreamed of in our own culture! [5]

In order to supply all the goods needed for these feasts, it was necessary to find more labor than the average family could furnish. Since the idea of paying for services had never entered into this tribal economy, the method of securing workers was to capture slaves. Instead of going to war for adventure or raiding for horses, as the Plains Indians did, these people took long canoe trips for the purpose of kidnapping unwary women and children. Frequently their captors used them, or, if they did not want them, they were sold or given away at *potlatches*. These slaves were quite well treated; they lived in the large house with their masters and worked with them. Sometimes they married into the tribe that they served, but it was always remembered if a person had slave ancestry. They often belonged to the highest class in their own tribes, but that did not help them any, except that occasionally, if their people located them, a trade was made for them. Even today slave ancestry is not forgotten.

The ceremonial life of the Northwest was colorful and unique in the pageant of American Indian life. They needed no dances for rain, but they had great gatherings to watch a medicine man cure the sick. They helped with the singing and watched with awe his summoning of his spirits. During the winter the guardian spirits that each person possessed came back to him. In order to appease them, the people gathered and helped a "sick" man sing his spirit "out" so that it could go on with its journey over the world and the "sick" man could live through another year with renewed vigor. These spirit visits conveniently came after the summer season of fishing and root gathering, when plenty of food was at hand for the inevitable feasting that accompanied all such affairs. Farther to the north the Kwakiutl, Haida, and Tsimshian had very elaborate ceremonials through their secret societies. By contrast the simple spirit singing of the Puget Sound Indians seems rather colorless, but anyone who has seen it feels that its sincerity is easily as satisfying as the theatrical showmanship of the North.

This all too brief summary of American Indian life points out just a few of the highlights of the varied ways of living practised by the original inhabitants of this continent. Many lessons can be learned from it. Everywhere the Indian adapted himself to the environment in which he lived and developed an integrated and harmonious life within the functioning social unit. It was, therefore, a serious matter when the white man appeared and destroyed any one part of this pattern. When through the introduction of new goods, desires were created that the old economy could not satisfy, people were torn from their old ways of living and families were disrupted. When white settlers moved into the great plains and slaughtered and scattered the buffalo herds, the Indians could no longer live their own life. People do not turn easily from the free life of a hunter to the settled routine of a farmer. Together with the disappearance of the basic economy, the very acts that brought social prestige and esteem to a man could no longer be carried out. In this depleted and transitional stage the Indians have been suspended for a century or more, the character and degree of the change depending on the region under discussion.

Many well intentioned programs have been developed to help the people adjust themselves to the new conditions, but since each region presents a different situation, these national plans have not always been well adapted to the need. Today many Indian groups have found a place for themselves in the white communities where they live. This means usually abandoning almost completely their old economy and many customs; but it is to be hoped that with a clearer understanding of the spiritual values of their older forms of life many of their concepts can be used as a basis for their present-day living. There was much in American Indian culture that was fine and on a high plane. A real effort should be made to salvage those ideas that are constructive for today's world without seeking to restore what has already been abandoned.

REFERENCES

For an extended treatment of Indian culture areas in North America see *The American Indian: An Introduction to the Anthropology of the New World*, by Clark Wissler. Third edition. New York, Oxford University Press, 1938.

1. "Aboriginal Culture of the Southeast," by John R. Swanton, in the *42nd Annual Report of the Bureau of American Ethnology*, 1924, pp. 677-726.
2. "Ethnographic Bibliography of North America," by George P. Murdock, in *Yale Anthropological Studies*, Vol. I. New Haven, Yale University Press, 1941.
3. "Where Did the Plains Indians Get Their Horses?" by Francis Haines, in *American Anthropologist*, Vol. 40, No. 1, 1938, pp. 112-117.
4. *First Penthouse Dwellers of America*, by Ruth M. Underhill. New York, J. J. Augustin, Inc., 1938.
5. For a different interpretation of the economic and social features of the *potlatch*, see Chapter VI.

Chapter III

INDIAN-WHITE RELATIONS

by Flora Warren Seymour

THE EARLY EUROPEAN COMER TO THESE SHORES DID not for a moment question his right to a foothold upon the new continent. Here was a vast region, sparsely inhabited by groups of semi-nomadic pagans who lived more by the chase than by agriculture, in a state of unremitting warfare one with another. Clearly it was more than a right; it was a duty to introduce to these peoples Christianity and civilization. Discovery, exploration, and settlement gave the newcomers a three-fold title that no court of law would ever question.

In the European sovereign, however, the legal title to the new lands rested. It was the Crown who granted to subjects the right to explore or colonize. With the natives remained the right of occupancy—a right recognized in court decisions. Thus the settler might acquire land by conquest or purchase, or possibly by an enforced combination of the two. As the Cherokees who by the Sycamore Shoals Treaty of 1775 sold Henderson the Kentucky country advised him, "Brother, you have bought a fair land, but you will find it hard to hold," so often the land purchased with gold and goods had to be defended with blood and sorrow. The red man had no such approach to the question of land ownership as had the white man. Land was not to him a permanent possession, but a region over which his tribe roamed in search of game or in warfare. He sold no more than he deemed himself to possess—the right of his group to hunt there until some stronger group drove them out.

This was the fundamental error at the bottom of the long series of purchases and treaties by which the white man sought to take peaceful possession. The European of the sixteenth or seventeenth century—no student of social development—read his own feelings into the aboriginal American, and acted accordingly.

In the same way he seemed to recognize in the almost formless groupings of the native the trappings of his own courts. It was an Indian "princess" who gave DeSoto a string of pearls. Powhatan, coming down the James in his dugout canoe, was an "emperor," and his lively little garmentless daughter, turning cartwheels on the sandy beach, was to become Mrs. John Rolfe, to be called "the Lady Rebecca," and to give the great Queen of England an anxious moment lest Mrs. Rolfe's admirers should accord her equal rank.

Indian "chiefs," in truth, are much more the creation of the white man than of the red.[1] Such leadership as Indians recognized was for warfare and had no relation to peace. But to do business spokesmen became necessary; or at least the European thought so. He picked out leaders who should receive the guns and powder, the blankets and calico, the trinkets and beads and mirrors for which the red man bartered his wares. These chiefs could distribute the goods among the people as they wished.

One sees the process beginning almost with the coming of the first Spanish caravels. Sir William Johnson, superintendent of Indians for the British Crown, described in detail his process of choosing chiefs, binding them to his interest.[2] A century later, United States employment of his methods is plain enough in the choosing of Oshkosh to represent the Menominees, or Keokuk among the Sac and Fox. Yet to this day there lingers in popular belief the false idea of Indians as ruled by chiefs.

The United States inherited the difficulties of a long colonial period. As the new nation grew it was to add many more. During somewhat more than the first half of our national existence, peaceful dealings with the Indian tribes were carried on by way of treaties, at first under the theory that the Indians were separate nations, and later under the power granted Congress to "regulate commerce" with the Indian tribes.

Even in colonial times the fiction of Indian nations was wearing thin. The Iroquois, who had the nearest approach to governmental organizations, were quite independent tribes, for all their council fires. And ever the dependence of red man upon white became more obvious. For while gun and powder and ball had transformed his life, the red man could not reproduce these for hunt and war. He did not learn to make repairs, but must petition for a blacksmith to keep his weapons in order.

Backed up by his "British father" at Fort Malden, Tecumseh, in the first decade of the nineteenth century, essayed the ambitious task of uniting many dissimilar tribes in warfare. At the close of the war in which he gave his life for England, the British peace commissioners suggested that an Indian nation be created in the "Northwest Territory." The American veto of this idea was unhesitating.[3] If Indians were to have a political organization, it would not be supervised from across the Atlantic.

THE CONCENTRATION POLICY

The vision of an Indian state, however, was strong with our forefathers of a century or so ago. Beyond the Mississippi, there could be established a gathering place for many tribes, to govern themselves and eventually develop into a state. This plan of concentration dominated United States policy on through the middle years of the century, until the idea of the Indian as "driven west" has become another of our national misapprehensions. The removal to the banks of the Arkansas River of the Southeastern groups known as the Five Civilized Tribes was a lively issue in those days, and the smoke and heat generated by that debate tended to gather around all Indian matters for many a year.

During this contest Supreme Court decisions were rendered that have influenced Indian relations ever since. Most notable was Chief Justice Marshall's dictum that the Indians were not foreign sovereignties, but "domestic dependent nations." [4] This was a new classification in law; domesticity and dependence are characteristics incompatible with the usual idea of nationality. Phrased more simply, this meant that the Indians, still taking care of their own affairs within the tribes, were legally incapable of handling affairs outside. They could not enter into treaty relations with any other country, nor could they dispose of their rights of land occupancy to any other nation or individuals.

One would naturally conclude that a group so situated was in no position to make a treaty with the United States, the inequality between the contracting parties being so marked. Yet treaty-making was to go on until the administration of President Grant.

As the years passed, more and more tribes came within the borders of the nation. When mid-century found the United

States fixed in its present continental boundaries, there was a wide expanse of white-dominated country east of the Mississippi and Missouri, a rapidly growing Pacific fringe, and between the two a region where many tribes roamed and hunted and resented the travel of the westering pioneers through the lands they knew.

This, then, was America's ultimate frontier—not the Pacific coast, but the plains, plateau, and mountain regions. Here were the last stands of many tribes, who set the fighting power in which they gloried against the small groups of traveling whites, unable to realize that behind these few pressed greater and greater hordes. The century was nearly done before the last of the Indian wars was ended.

But amid the war-making, there was growing up the movement to bring the Indian into civilization as an individual. The treaties, by setting boundaries to roaming and hunting grounds, had thus created "reservations," as the lands reserved for Indian occupancy were called. The hope was that there should be use as well as occupancy; that the Indian would learn to live by the soil, as the white man had done. For America was still markedly agricultural. Love of the land had been the deep underlying motive of the great migrations across this vast continent. Again reading into the red man's mind his own impulses, the white man assumed that the Indian, too, clung to the soil and depended upon it.

THE ALLOTMENT POLICY

Therefore, so the white man reasoned, if the Indian had an individual piece of land, his own allotment, secured to him by law, he would build his life and his livelihood about it. Having the means of self-support, he would become self-supporting. Through all his contact with the white race, the Indian had thought of his claim to the land merely as somehing that could be brought forward as a demand for pres- nts, annuities, and rations. Yet now it was assumed that he vould at once take the reasoned attitude of the homesteader. With the exception of the village Indians of the Southwest, none of the tribes had developed a farm economy. Many of he buffalo-hunting groups raised no agricultural products whatever. In other sections the women did a little planting of corn and beans and the like. But only in those few small ettled groups who had had long contact with the Spanish ettlers did the men do any tilling of the soil.

Early trials of allotment showed that it is easier to change a legal status than a mental outlook. There were instances where individual titles were granted, as in the case of the ndians of Michigan, whose long admixture of white blood and long contact with white life should have given them ome insight into the value of land. Yet when these part- ndians received title to individual farms, it was all but uni- versally the case that they sold at the first offer.

Those who advocated allotment—and among them were many of the most devoted friends the red men ever had— now added to the demand for land in severalty the proviso hat for a number of years the land should be held in trust by the government, its sale forbidden. At the end of this period it was to go to the Indian owner without encumbrance, a property free from debt and all his own. The intervening years were to be a time of training in citizenship and indus- ry. Eventually the period of trust was set at twenty-five years, evidently too long for an educational program. Yet with such proviso the General Allotment Act, or Dawes Act, was finally passed.[5]

This Act provided for the making of allotments as each ribe was judged to have reached a suitable degree of civiliza- tion. Unfortunately, enthusiasm often outweighed caution, and in the thirty years following the passage of the Act a great proportion of the reservations were divided up into allotments. If there was land remaining, it was to be sold and the proceeds used for the erection of houses and the purchase of the materials, machines, and work animals that would set a man up as a farmer. This sale of "surplus" land was one of the things that in recent years has been represented as a systematic despoiling of Indian lands by the rapacious and cruel white man. It should be noted that the sales were of land over and above what was supposed to be a sufficient allotment for each individual; and that the proceeds of the sales were by no means lost, but dedicated to Indian use. A reservation in which allotments have been made and the surplus land offered for sale is an open reservation. There are many reservations still "closed," in the sense that the land has not yet been given out to individuals, the Navajo reservation in New Mexico and Arizona being an example.

While the purpose of allotting lands individually was to educate the Indian in self-support, several modifications of the original law took place almost immediately. These had the result of weakening the good intent of the Act, if not absolutely defeating it. Thus it was provided that the allottee should, on receiving his trust patent, become a citizen of the United States and of the state in which he lived, subject to the laws, both civil and criminal, of both jurisdictions. Three or four years later an amendment wiped out the portion requiring obedience to state laws; [6] to this day a great number of Indians, with or without allotments, are free from obedience to the laws binding upon their fellow-citizens, and are even officially advised to disregard certain enactments.[7]

INDIAN ACT OF CANADA

In contrast to this is the "Indian Act" of Canada, which provides for the withdrawal of an Indian from his wardship status if a board declares him fit to undertake life unsupervised. If his application for "enfranchisement" is approved, his lands, previously assigned to his use by the tribe, are given to him in fee simple. He pays the tribe for its interest in these lands; and at the same time receives his proportionate share of tribal moneys. Two years later his enfranchisement is deemed complete. His property becomes subject to taxation and he is assured of "all the legal powers, rights, and privileges of His Majesty's other subjects."[8] Thereafter, he is no longer an Indian within the meaning of the Act.

In contrast to this clean break with old relations and assumption of a new status, allotment in the United States left the relationship much less clearly defined; and subsequent modifications of the Act had still greater effect in retarding Indian development.

ADVENT OF THE LEASING SYSTEM

Thus, the idea of the allotment as a farm involved family ownership. The expectation was that a family should reside upon a farm, make their living therefrom, and hand it down to a son for the use of the next generation. With this idea in mind one or two reservations, as with the Oneida in Wisconsin, were divided on the basis of a certain number of acres for the head of a family, and a smaller number for young people who would presumably be founding families of their own. But before long it became apparent that the alleged looseness of marital ties, and in particular the polygamous relations common within a number of tribes, made it quite uncertain that allotment to a man made any provision for his wife or wives. Besides, a great argument was raised that everyone should receive an allotment. The use of the land was forgotten; ownership loomed up as the only desideratum. Accordingly, the rule was adopted to give everyone equal acreage. Old people and infants, hale men and invalids, even people who died in the course of the roll-making, were assigned equal shares.

This rule meant that an Indian family, instead of owning one farm, held title to a varying number of farms, most of which they could not possibly use. The practical answer to this problem unfortunately involved the creation of another of those evils that have been brought upon the red man with all good intentions for his welfare. Where the land was worth using, white men stood ready to lease it; and after various shifts the law finally settled down to permitting the lease of an Indian's land, whether he himself was or was not able to use it. The government handled the business details at no expense to the owner. No one can wonder that he too frequently preferred to become a landlord, rather than to earn a livelihood by the sweat of his brow. Even if he had not still clung, in many cases, to the primitive scorn of tilling the soil, he would be of superhuman fortitude to choose to get by the hard way what he might receive without effort.

So allotment too often simply confirmed the Indian in the idea that had been created in the old treaty days. Ownership of the land still meant no more than an opportunity to get something from others, and not out of the soil itself. Consequently, when the Indian became legally competent to sell his land, it is not surprising that his first impulse was to barter it off for anything that took his fancy, whether or not of equal value. The educational purpose of allotment had been practically forgotten; nothing in his experience had taught him the real value of the land.

It had been assumed that making the new allottee a citizen would make him a taxpayer as well. Instead, it was not long before the courts decided that the land must emerge from the trust period entirely without encumbrance, even to the extent of taxes.

Again the material estate of the Indian was to benefit at the expense of his morale. And in the mind of the public there grew up the idea that for some reason based on his possible possession of some aboriginal blood, the red man was to be forever free from civic obligations.

IMPLICATIONS OF WARDSHIP

Both Canadian and United States law had long forbidden the sale or gift of liquor to an Indian or within Indian country. The Canadian liquor ban did not apply to an enfranchised Indian; while in the United States in the early days of allotment the Indian who had attained citizenship was formally adjudged by the courts to be possessed of the right to walk into a saloon and call for fire water.

For some years this situation existed; then a decision in 1916 reversed the decree and prohibition laws were held to apply even to an Indian citizen. The theory was thus established that it is possible for an Indian to be at the same time citizen and ward. An Indian might be a voter in the state and at the same time exempt from obedience to its laws. He was to have the restrictions as well as the privileges of wardship despite his status as a citizen.

But before this second decision, the Congress of the United States had taken other action in amendment of the General Allotment Act. By a measure passed in 1906, known as the Burke Act, it was provided that in allotments made thereafter, citizenship should be reserved until the trust period was over and the final title, or patent in fee, was issued.

Already, however, a substantial proportion of the red men had become citizens. Under this Act or other laws and treaties, fully two-thirds of the Indians of the United States were citizens before the passage of the Act of 1924 granting citizenship to all born within our borders. All are now citizens, and the co-existent wardship is a matter of so many restrictions and exemptions, so many decisions of varying applicability, that citizenship is thus hemmed in by a vast cloud of uncertainty. Clarification of the situation is urgently needed.

Among other features of the Burke Act was a provision that, if an Indian proved himself competent to handle his own affairs, he need not wait until the end of a twenty-five year trust period before being given full title to his land. Upon the showing of the allottee's physical and mental capacity, the Secretary of the Interior was authorized to issue a patent in fee.

COMPETENCY COMMISSIONS ESTABLISHED

At first this issuance of complete title went on individually and with no great speed. But a new policy, inaugurated when Franklin K. Lane was Secretary of the Interior, hastened the matter of dismissing land from supervision. Competency commissions were appointed to pass upon the qualifications of all holders of trust patents. If these allottees were found to be of good health and mentality, in the years of vigor and activity, English-speaking and educated, it was presumed that they should be able to assume full responsibility for their own property. Many such were found and patents in fee were issued.

The result was all too often an immediate sale. Health, strength, and school training did not necessarily give a man or woman economic wisdom, nor incline him or her to the life of a farmer. Nor is this failure to use the land and to appreciate its value as a capital asset to be attributed to any particularly Indian qualities. One has but to consider a moment what might be the effect if every man, woman, and child in a village were to receive an endowment of a farm. How large a proportion would, or could, take to farming? After those who were too old or too young, too feeble in mind or body, were set aside, would the eligible remnant take up the plow or reaper just because of the possession of property? How many would there be who would fail to do just what the larger proportion of the Indian owners did—sell the land and enjoy the proceeds?

The time of this new policy, be it remembered, was also that of World War I, when land was in greater demand for wheat growing than at any period in America's history. For the next few years land prices were to reach an all-time high. The temptation to sell was irresistible to many.

Later on these sales of land were also to figure as "losses," stigmatized by some as further instances of white greed. Nevertheless, it is probable that a dispassionate study would show that a great proportion of the lands sold could be purchased now for a much smaller sum than the Indians received back in the expansive twenties.

With the coming of a new administration this policy was abandoned, and as the twenties went on it was usually the case that when a tribe neared the end of the twenty-five year trust period, an executive order would be sought and obtained, extending the life of the trust for ten or fifteen years, or even another quarter-century. The educational purpose was now quite forgotten, since after a half-century of supervision as an incompetent there could be no expectation of development into competency.

Indians soon learned to think of this issuance of patents in fee as an injustice and an injury. An outcry against "forced patents" was raised and may still be heard from time to time. The term is applied commonly, now, to any receipt of authority to sell. Yet an analysis of the actual situation in any case may prove that full title to the land was by no means forced upon its owner.

THE CASE OF THE PAWNEES

A study made in the early thirties of the Pawnee allotment roll offers some revealing facts. This tribe, situated in north-central Oklahoma, received trust allotments in 1893, so that the expiration of the twenty-five year trust period coincided with the high land value period just following the First World War. Nevertheless, the trust was extended on many of the tracts of land that had been allotted. On the other hand, a considerable number of allottees received their fee patents and sold their lands for prices that seemed almost fabulous when the study was made, in a time of depression. In some cases the prevailing high land prices were augmented by the hope of oil discoveries.

Fifty allotments were chosen for an intensive study. The talk of "forced patents" was prevalent here, and attention was especially given to that point. The issuance of fee patents had indeed been general. The competency commission had listened to the requests of a great number of Indians, and had granted them. The interesting point was that in nearly every instance there was a justification that would seem reasonable to anyone. The allottee was old and needed the money. (It must be remembered that a large proportion would come in the upper age brackets, twenty-five years after allotment.) This one needed an operation; and at that time the government had not developed the free surgical service now available to Indians. That one was employed elsewhere, could not use the land, but could use the money to better his condition where he resided. So the stories ran. All the reasons seemed plausible and convincing.

In the cases studied only two instances were found of anything that could be termed a "forced" patent. These cases involved one young man and one young woman, both well educated, able-bodied, in the prime of life, only partly of Indian blood, both holding positions in government service. Their patents in fee were issued without application, on the theory that they had been prepared for the responsibility of full land ownership and were capable of undertaking it. If such young people as these disposed of their land and later regretted their action, they were in no sense forced to do so. Should such transactions be charged in the public consciousness as land losses due to white rapacity or betrayal of trust?

The lesson behind all this, obvious to the student, was entirely missed by the casual observer. It was plain that Indians in general did not have the view of the ownership and use of land that the white man assumed to be a common human characteristic. It was also evident that the Indians would not become one hundred per cent tillers of the soil, however much they possessed and under whatever title they possessed it. Yet the public, so far as it knew or cared anything about Indian matters, persisted in the impression, augmented by wide publicity from time to time, that the sole cause of difficulty was the defrauding of the Indian of his land, and that restoring land to him was the only way of expiating a crime as well as insuring his wealth and happiness.

ASSUMPTIONS OF THE NEW POLICY

A similar assumption underlay the legislative proposals of 1934, sponsored as a "self-government" bill. This bill of forty-eight pages prescribed a return to tribal life and to the status of incompetency from which the Indian had been trying to emerge. Under the provisions of this bill no Indian was ever to receive full title to his acreage. Indeed, the original proposal was to take the land from those who had received title in trust, and put it again into tribal and governmental ownership. This proposal was a complete violation of Constitutional principles. Indeed, it struck at the very foundation of English law. It assumed a power over land titles such as no British sovereign had ever claimed. Yet when this provision was deleted from the bill, the omission was less because of its patent illegality than because the Indians had made it plain that they would not relinquish their land. The framers of this legislation had thought of the red man as devoted to a communal ideal of all for one and one for all. They learned with surprise that while the Indian lacked European ideas of land ownership, he was quite as wholeheartedly individualistic as any product of civilization.

Much public protest arose over this bill, the greater share from the Indians themselves. In its final form, one-fourth the original size, many of the dubious provisions were omitted.[9] Enough remained, however, to mark a serious change in Indian policy. The Indian Office now declares it deals with the tribes rather than with the Indian as an individual.

The sale of Indian lands has been banned. The issuance of allotments is forbidden. Much land has been purchased by the government to be added to Indian reservations. The possibility of such "enfranchisement" as Canadian law permits is not considered.

For dealing with Indians tribally an elaborate machinery has been instituted. First it was provided that the tribes should vote separately on the matter of accepting the new law. Some have adopted the plan; others have rejected it despite a vast amount of persuasion and inducement in the way of various subsidies. The next step was to be the formation of a constitution. Finally, it was expected that the tribe would proceed to the organization of a corporation, with a charter and the right to borrow money from the government and enter into business, which would thus be termed a "cooperative." Needless to say, every step of this procedure was to be taken by and with the consent and advice of the Secretary of the Interior.

This procedure, which has in some cases been followed through the various contemplated steps, has for the most part resulted in a cooperation no more actual than that of a stockholder who receives a dividend from a share of Standard Oil stock that has been given him. Technically he may be said to be helping to manage the affairs of the company, but his actual cooperation in anything except a share of the profits is rather remote.

REVIVAL OF TRIBALISM

By this intricate legalistic web the Indian is understood to be returning to the tribal autonomy that his fathers were presumed to enjoy. The legislation, after being called the Self-Government Act, was later known as the Organization Act. More recently this has been changed to the Re-organization Act, to emphasize the idea that it is a restoration of the tribal government that Indians once enjoyed. To anyone even slightly acquainted with their history, comparison of the present complicated entanglement with their free, almost governmentless existence is farcical indeed.

The logic of present events, likewise, is all in opposition to continued segregation. The blood mixture that began in the days of Columbus has gone on progressively, until it would be impossible to prove that there is any so-called Indian within our country whose tribe and family group

have not received at some period a non-Indian strain. Th
regulations concerning Indians more and more apply to peopl
of small degree of Indian blood, whose continuing adaptatio
to white ways is a matter of generations if not of centurie
It is unnatural to require them to remain primitive in th
face of such undeniable development.

The Canadian Indian Act provides that an Indian wh
absents himself for five years from its jurisdiction withou
consent of the Superintendent General ceases to be an India
within the meaning of the Act. An Indian woman marryin
a white man loses her Indian status, receiving her share o
tribal funds on her dismissal. It is also provided that the ban
exclude illegitimate children from its rolls and benefits. Thu
in various ways the northern Dominion provides legally fo
the continual seepage into the white race. It is much mor
realistic than United States law, which ignores the constan
increase of white blood.

A PRESENT-DAY ANOMALY

Legally, the present situation of the American Indian i
strangely anomalous. He is a citizen of the United States, an
at the same time is in that position "analogous to wardship"
of which Chief Justice Marshall spoke a century ago. Whil
Marshall referred to the tribe rather than the individual, th
business of government oversight has been carried on fo
both individuals and groups until it is the assumption o
white and red men alike that the mere possession of a smal
portion of Indian blood in his veins entitles a citizen to an
number of more or less vaguely defined restrictions and exemptions.

Thus, while he moves among white men, he is subject t
the laws that govern them. But on restricted land, that is
land still held in trust by the government, he is not subjec

o the laws of the state. For a murder committed on the eservation he is answerable to a Federal court; for one comnitted in the near-by town, he may be taken in hand by the ocal authorities. And of course there can be a nice case of urisdiction brought up to complicate the inquiry into the rime itself.

In lesser matters, domestic relations and the like, he is, n the reservation, independent of state law. In 1934, as reviously noted, the Hopis were officially advised that nothng required them to obey the Arizona statute as to marriage nd divorce. Following their own rather casual and informal rocedure in such matters, a number of the young men of he Hopi tribe in the armed forces are now finding it dificult to give any substantial evidence of a marriage relation table enough to justify claims for their families.

At the same time, though frequently exempt from obedince to state laws, many Indians are voters and help to choose he lawmakers of the state. In Arizona and New Mexico ertain groups of Indians are excluded from suffrage on the round of their wardship relation to the Federal government nd their exemption from taxpaying; but in most of the tates Indians enjoy suffrage under the same conditions as ther citizens. Thus, in the Dakotas an Indian might vote for nembers of the state legislature, might indeed even himself e elected to that lawmaking body, and yet, on returning to is home on the reservation, be without responsibility to obey he law that he himself had helped to make.

In the United States, compulsory elementary school attendnce is enforced against all peoples except the Indians, who lone have special government schools provided for them. t may be added that some states, such as South Dakota, have ompulsory school laws for Indians as well as other citizens. By Canadian law the Indian band enforces school attendance between the ages of seven and fifteen, or until the elementary grades are completed. Indian parents not complying with the law may suffer fine or imprisonment for their failure.

While lands held in trust are untaxable, other property owned by Indians of the United States may be subject to taxation. Here again is a twilight zone in which the Indian's status varies in a manner to confuse citizens much more experienced than he in legalities.

WHO IS AN INDIAN?

And indeed the very question as to who is or is not an Indian is a matter of great perplexity. There are owners of trust allotments who do not possess even a trace of Indian blood, descendants of white captives or freed slaves. There are others whose claimed percentage of Indian blood is so little that the connection with a tribe is all but non-existent. Allottees who must go back six to ten generations to find a completely Indian ancestor certainly have a very slight claim upon the racial name. The idea that so distant a connection should exempt them from obedience to the law, for example, is preposterous. Yet so completely is the whole matter of Indianism beclouded, both historically and legally, that the attempt to make a definition is beset with many difficulties. It is obvious, however, that some boundary should be set, beyond which the claim to special treatment should be ruled out.

Of recent years the use of the term wardship has been somewhat discouraged officially. It has come to mean both so much and so little that the phrase does not recommend itself to careful usage. But the fact of Indian dependence upon Federal supervision is ever more and more emphasized. The whole effect of recent legislation is to draw the net more tightly about those known as Indians, to segregate them more nd more from their white brothers on the other side of an .lmost imaginary dividing line.

That this segregation works hardships as well as good is ncreasingly obvious. If there is any benefit to the Indian in ıot being bound by the state laws, it is outweighed by the ttitude this exemption creates both in himself and in his vhite fellow-citizens, who cannot fail to think of him as a ›erson below the level of law observance. If he is relieved ·f the payment of taxes on his land, he pays intangibly for he relief in the lowered esteem of citizens who do their part n maintaining local government. And both in the minds of ıis neighbors, who resent his freedom from obligations, and n the hearts of those who sentimentally implore for him ;reater benefits, he becomes stigmatized as the perpetual ecipient of public funds for which no return is to be given.

It is a stigma from which many of the race wish to be elieved. The Navajos, for example, are accounted among the nore primitive of the tribes. Yet they understand well the ıature of the prejudice created by government subsidy. In ·lanning the purchase of extra lands with tribal funds, they ıave petitioned that they may hold these lands subject to he taxation of the state.[10] Their equality with other citizens ; more valuable to them than the saving that nonpayment ·f taxes would bring.

It has been possible to touch upon only the highlights in he vast picture of the red man's legal situation. So far as ·lood content is concerned, Indian assimilation is proceeding :onstantly, rapidly, inescapably. Moreover, adaptation to American life is going on with equal speed, despite efforts to ıold back the advance in order that aspiring antiquarians may ›e occupied or curiosity-seeking tourists may be titillated. To .ttempt the restoration of Indian culture is the most futile of endeavors, since culture in its very nature involves change. Any culture that can be arrested and fixed in its mold is dead and no longer the possession of living human beings.

Yet this modern Indian, who probably has more white ancestors than red, who is perhaps of the third generation among his Indian forebears to enjoy educational benefits, who is indubitably a citizen and in most instances a voter, is still bound like Gulliver in a tangle of Lilliputian laws and regulations. It is not surprising that his movements are often hampered and his strength weakened. The day should not be far distant when he will stand erect, call his muscles into play, and achieve the freedom Americans prize.

REFERENCES

1. "Fiction of Indian Chiefs," pp. 52-53, in *The Scientific American*, July, 1935.
2. *The Sir William Johnson Papers;* nine volumes published at varying dates at Albany, by the University of the State of New York.
3. *Diary of John Quincy Adams, 1794-1845,* edited by Allan Nevins, pp. 123 ff. New York, Longmans, Green and Co. 1929.
4. Cherokee v. Georgia. 5 Pet. 1 (1831).
5. 24 Stat. 388, Feb. 8, 1887.
6. 26 Stat. 794, Feb. 28, 1891.
7. Circular to the Hopi, November 9, 1934. See also section on Law and Order in *Indian Wardship*, pp. 18-19, issued by the Home Missions Council, New York, N. Y., 1943.
8. Sec. 110, The Indian Act. Rev. Stat. of Canada, vol. 2, ch. 98. Ottawa, 1927.
9. 48 Stat. 984, June 18, 1934.
10. Gallup (N. M.) *Gazette*, December 24, 1942.

Chapter IV

ADJUSTING TO SOCIAL CHANGE

THAT INDIANS OF THE OLD TRAIL WAGED A HARSH struggle for existence in which the mere act of survival often became an hourly triumph over fate is a well attested fact. Champlain, the intrepid, early-day explorer whose contact with the red men was intimate, phrases it as follows: "Their existence is miserable as compared with ours, but it is satisfactory to them because they have not tasted better, and because they believe that there is none more desirable. They are content among themselves, having no other ambition than to keep alive."[1]

This is a far cry from those to whom the old Indian life appears to have been idyllic and who bemoan the passing of the carefree tribalism of the pre-Columbian era when game was plentiful, wild fruits, roots, and herbs abounded, and social as well as economic security lay within reach of all. However, the painstaking work of eminent research students of the past reveals no such Golden Age. In fact, they aver that whatever Golden Age the Indians may have enjoyed was the era of trading with the whites. That was the "period of great economic prosperity for the Indian."[2] That the fur trade increased the larder of the Indian as well as that of the trader, few will question. Oliver Faribault, a noted fur trader, used to say that he counted it a loss of five hundred dollars for every Indian who learned to read and write.

But in the face of white expansion the Indian could n
rely for his subsistence on the chase. It was only a questic
of time before the buffalo was wiped out and the Plai
Indian called upon to make new adjustments. His nomadis
came to an abrupt end; nor could he forever rely upc
rations. He must at least be exposed to some of the rur
experiences of him who "tills a lonely field to reap its scant
corn." In short, the one-time warrior and hunter was calle
upon to learn the dignity of labor, that "the first farmer w
the first man, and that all historic nobility rests on possessio
and use of land."

CHANGE TO A LAND ECONOMY

Needless to say, this transition was not an easy one. It w
considered beneath the dignity of the hunter and warrior t
engage in manual labor. Planting, cultivation of the field, an
even harvesting were tasks generally assumed by womer
though by no means a universal procedure. Then, too, amon
certain tribes the earth was thought of as their mother an
there was a marked aversion toward using hoe or spade i
injuring her surface. Had not Mother Earth been graciou
in supplying wild fruit and nuts without cultivation? More
over, in the Pacific Northwest a cult known as "Dreamers'
held it a sacrilege to mar the landscape by plowshare o
pruning-hook. Some believed that certain epidemics wer
due to the white man's cultivation of the soil.

There were some striking exceptions to this general rule
The village dwellers of the Southwest, especially the Pueblos
Zuñis, Hopis, and Pimas, were already agriculturalists. The
were, for the most part, peaceful, stay-at-home people, wh
for unknown generations had fought nature on their semi
arid deserts. Some of them practised irrigation long befor
the advent of the white man.

In the Southwest, too, are the Navajos, now the largest of all the tribes, living on a reservation the size of several New England states. Once feared as raiders, they are known in our day as the most successful land group operators among Indians, wresting a living from the soil where few white men would attempt it. This does not mean that they are "dirt farmers" as that term is usually understood. They do, however, plant corn, melons, and other field crops wherever nature has permitted enough water to gather in their desert land. But their main dependence has been, and still is, sheep and goats. Navajo women have excelled in rug weaving and some of the men have become proficient in silversmithing and kindred crafts.

Only a few years ago these same people, whom Kit Carson once called "the hardy, industrious Navajo," were suddenly subjected to a radical sheep and goat reduction program, having as its aim the control of soil erosion. This effort was coupled with the introduction of a wage economy program. Both of these left the Navajos confused and uncertain. Back of these attempts lay a lack of knowledge of the Navajos and of sympathetic understanding of the human issues involved in carrying out experiments in soil erosion control. Almost overnight, Navajo land was called upon to bridge the gap between a nomadic shepherd economy and a modern wage economy. Under the old manner of life the women own the sheep, weave the blankets, trade and barter; and usually they make both ends meet. The new situation meant that the men were employed on various relief projects at sixty dollars a month and that they thus became very wage-conscious. At once they were exposed to influences demanding a standard of living far removed from that symbolized by the *hogan* fare of mutton and black coffee.

It is not our purpose to discuss here the various attempts

to fit the Indian into a land economy. Suffice it to say that his career as an agriculturalist has been a checkered one. Whether agriculture is his most important means of subsistence is a moot question. To assume that all Indians must farm is folly; the assumption that no Indian makes a good farmer is equally wrong. The fact remains that while Indian land holdings are limited,[3] the amount of land still held is sufficient to afford each Indian approximately one hundred and sixty acres per capita.[4] Of course, much of this might be classed by land appraisers as arid, swampy, mountainous, and otherwise unproductive. The latter is especially true in California, where Indians were assigned scattered public domain allotments, generally worthless, or other equally meager holdings where they rarely had enough land to earn individual livings. A similar situation obtains among certain Nevada groups. However, the total area still in Indian ownership causes one to wonder whether the thesis that has been so widely publicized of recent years, that "the Indian's master problem is land," [5] can really be taken seriously.

Land itself is only potential wealth. The use made of the land is what counts in the final analysis. If land and the possession of the fruits of the land, such as natural resources, including oil, minerals, and timber, would bring "racial salvation," then certainly such tribes as the Osages, Klamaths, Menominees, and Quapaws should be the happiest, most contented and "racially saved" people on earth. Unfortunately, this condition does not obtain.

TRANSITION IN CANADA

In Canada the basic Indian pursuits of hunting and fishing have been powerfully influenced not only by early European contacts, but more especially by the fur trade of the Hudson's Bay Company. Trade relations continued virtually uninterrupted for centuries, and this relationship ceased only when the right to the land passed to the Canadian government and the lords of the plains became the wards of the government. Even today in the wilder regions life is still on a primitive scale and hunting the principal means of livelihood. Looking at a map of these vast spaces it is difficult to realize that the supply of game is diminishing. In fact, in some provinces, notably Quebec, several reserves of territory have been set aside in recent years for the benefit of those tribes dwelling in the forest region and designated as "Indian Hunting Ground."

However, the agency that has broken the isolation of the Indians in the prairie provinces has been the Canadian Pacific Railway. With the coming of settlers to make homes where once the buffalo roamed, the red man, placed on reserves on the basis of six hundred and forty acres to each family of five, or one hundred and twenty-eight acres for each individual, soon found himself directed toward such agricultural pursuits as stock raising and diversified farming.

PROGRESS IN AGRICULTURE

What progress has been made in stimulating the Indian to take up agricultural pursuits? Twenty years ago the U. S. Indian Bureau pointed with pride to 50,000 Indians who were cultivating a million acres or more, while 44,000 were engaged in the stock-raising industry; 27,000 were listed as following other pursuits, including, for instance, such handicrafts as blanket and basket weaving, bead-work, pottery, and similar occupations.[6] Since then drought and depression have left their toll of victims among Indians as well as whites. Great numbers were thrown upon relief, either direct relief or so-called "made work" projects, such as road building, timber restoration and conservation, and similar projects. In many respects this marked a period of poverty and low incomes perhaps unparalleled in recorded Indian history.

A turn for the better has come in very recent years, but whether this is due to more normal climatic conditions and better prices, or whether the relatively large sums released as "credit loans" by the Indian Office are a factor, may be open to question.[7] While comparable figures covering two decades are not available, it may be of interest to note that in 1923 Indian farmers numbered 40,962, and they were cultivating 890,700 acres of land. The value of all cattle owned by Indians at that time was estimated at $35,000,000.[8] In 1940 the number of Indians owning beef cattle is reported as 16,624. Livestock owned by Indians is distributed as follows: beef cattle, 262,551; dairy cattle, 39,375; sheep and goats, 802,603; swine, 43,496; poultry, 645,929; horses and mules, 133,067. The value of all livestock owned totals $18,849,279, while the amount received from the sale of all livestock and products totals $5,859,299. When it comes to the actual cultivation of the soil, the record is not encouraging, for we learn that the acreage of field crops harvested was 595,440, while the production of forage crops was 279,626 tons, that of cereal crops, 2,970,957 bushels, potatoes, 192,747 bushels.[9]

The foregoing recital would seem to indicate that stock raising offers a greater appeal to the Indian than the more prosaic tasks incidental to tilling the soil. He makes a good cowboy, for he is fond of horses; the annual round-ups and rodeos seldom lack for Indian support and participation. Perhaps the most promising features of latter-day reservation activities, where grazing lands abound, are the cattlemen's associations, managed to a certain extent by the Indians themselves.

The Blood Reserve near Cardston, Alberta, approximately

hirty by sixty miles in extent and said to be the largest in he Dominion, exhibits a fair example of progress in agricul- ure and stock raising on the part of buffalo-hunting Indians of a generation or two ago. Here one may meet progressive farmers with well tended cattle herds, with milch cows as well as a limited supply of hogs and poultry. Of course, the pres- ence of horses, mostly range animals, often eating more than they are worth, is a carry-over from the past, when wealth consisted largely in the number of horses owned. The use of modern combines indicates that wheat and small grains are the main dependence in this and other typical prairie reserves.

MODERN TRENDS

But what about those who do not take readily to rural life, whether it be plowing the field or riding the range? For obviously one cannot expect all Indians to become farmers and stockmen. Not long ago in one of the larger vocational government schools, which specializes in agriculture, 428 boys were asked to give their choice of industrial training. Of these, 282 elected such courses as auto mechanics, welding, and sheet-metal work, although agriculture courses were required the first year. In this, of course, they do not vary greatly from average American youth of the present day. Contributing factors are the static conditions inherent in reservation life, the delayed pay-check, loneliness after group living in the boarding schools, and the pauperization that has too often characterized these "government almshouses," as someone has characterized the reservations. To them the more aggressive Indian youth are reluctant to return.

With the general spread of education and increasing contacts with fellow-citizens of other groups, the lure of the outside world, with the promise of more gainful employment, has asserted itself. Today it can be said that the cream of

Indian youth tend to establish themselves in organized towns and cities. In a recent survey (1941) of the Oneidas of Wisconsin, it was found that fully one-half of the 3,394 on the annuity roll were living away from the reservation. The same can be said of the Santee Sioux of Nebraska, as well as of other tribal groups. A number of these have positions in the Indian Service as teachers, matrons, nurses, mechanics, clerks, foremen.

In 1938, more than 50 per cent of the 8,500 employees in the Indian Service were Indians and the percentage is still increasing, according to Miss Edna A. Gerken, specialist in adult education.[10] A rapidly increasing number of young men and women are in positions of responsibility, involving skill and a knowledge of high standards of work and of professional ethics. They are occupying, by and large, positions open to any other citizen, regardless of race or creed. Many not only are earning a living but at the same time are bringing up children, well cared for and well behaved, in homes that have frequently more than the necessities of life.

A survey of Indians in urban life made by the writer[11] a few years ago revealed that a certain midwestern urban center provided a place where Indians lived independently in the ordinary community and where assimilation had been going forward for a considerable period; that there were no segregated Indian residential districts; that "Indianism" as such was not capitalized nor commercialized—the gaily bedecked headdresses and ceremonial dress were seen only at show time; that there were no segregated Indian schools, government or private; that many people of Indian blood were not "race-conscious," although they did not hesitate to point with pride to their Indian lineage at the annual banquet of the Indian club; that every one of the well known welfare agencies reported, "We do not have any Indian families among our clients at the present time, or, if we have, we do not recognize them as such."[12]

To the question, Is it possible for the Indian to become adjusted to city life under modern conditions?, the answer is virtually the same as the one given to the oft-repeated query, Is it possible to civilize an Indian? The Indian can become adjusted to urban life even as he is becoming adjusted to modern civilization. Of course, those who would "foster the ancient traditions" may not welcome this viewpoint. It is possible to put too much emphasis on the fancied injustice of requiring the Indian to conform to changing conditions. This is far from saying, however, that every Indian should be urged to leave his rural community and exchange a precarious livelihood for what might easily prove to be a still more uncertain one in the city.

Indians in ever growing numbers, whether in rural or urban surroundings, increasingly realize that the road to economic success lies in work and thrift; there is the recognition, too, that even if Uncle Sam in a generous mood might hand out largess on a silver platter, more than satisfying "claims" to past hunting grounds, such benefactions would be impoverishing, not only to the Indian but to his children's children, for they do not lead to independence and self-respect.

HEALTH AND PHYSICAL WELL-BEING

Romance has pictured the Indian of the old trail as possessed of a bronzed body, inured to heat and cold, hunger and privation, of marked athletic propensities, his whole being vibrating with health and physical vitality. A story is told of a Yankee, traveling abroad, who on being shown a statue of Apollo exclaimed, "Well, I'll be jiggered if it ain't a Mohawk." Whether the North American Indians were in reality such perfect physical specimens, among whom the ravages of illness were practically unknown prior to the coming of the white man, is seriously open to question. Commenting on this, Dr. J. G. Townsend, former director of health in the United States Indian Service, says: "Certainly it is true that the diseases commonly affecting the white man had a fruitful habitat in the body of the American Indian when he met for the first time another race harboring these diseases." [13]

Between 1781 and 1840 smallpox made its rounds no less than three times in certain areas, ravaging entire tribes. It was more deadly in its effects than the Spanish influenza of World War I. Before immunization measures had developed, such epidemic diseases as measles took a heavy toll. Then, too, when Indians were first concentrated in restricted areas with meager sanitary facilities, there was a rapid rise in such diseases as colds, diphtheria, pneumonia, tuberculosis, and trachoma. At present, tuberculosis is still the great killer, while trachoma is all too prevalent despite remarkable results recently attained through the use of sulfa drugs.

In the early days, medical care was largely limited to what a few missionary doctors [14] and army surgeons were able to do. As a matter of fact, many tribes believed most sicknesses were caused by the activity of evil spirits, spirits that might lie in ambush, beside a shrub, tree, brook, or swamp, ready to wreak vengeance on the unsuspecting. Consequently, it became the duty of the medicine priest to lure away these spirits.

It is a far cry from the primitive sings and exorcisms of the medicine man to the treatment available for Indian patients today in modern reservation hospitals. Today not only Indian school children, but adults as well, receive more adequate medical care than a large percentage of the surrounding white population. There are to be found in the governıent Indian Service 78 general hospitals and 12 sanatoriums, vith a total of 4,528 beds and a medical personnel of nearly ,000 in the field.[15] Appropriations for these hospitals and anatoriums for the fiscal year ending June 30, 1943, amount o $5,551,936.[16]

In Canada, probably the earliest hospital devoted exclu-ively to the care of Indians was the Dynevor, opened in 1896 n the banks of the Red River near West Selkirk. Originally romoted by church agencies, it now receives an annual grant rom the government, supplemented by private subscriptions. n a number of reserves there are now similar hospitals, while he Indian Department provides field matrons, district nurses, nd contract doctors.

As in the United States, tuberculosis is the most frequent ause of death. To combat this, extensions for the accommo-lation of tubercular patients have been added to a number f hospitals, and in 1921 the Sarcee School in Alberta was onverted into a tubercular institution, being transferred to he Dominion government for that purpose. On the Pacific oast medical missions similar to the famous Grenfell Mis-ion of Labrador have been established. The steamers of the Columbia Coast Mission often are provided with hospital vards as well as dispensaries to meet the needs of lonely and solated Indian fishing villages.

In Alaska, hospital facilities have been provided for the Eskimo by church agencies, while the government has been argely responsible for medical services to the Indians in the outheastern region. Tuberculosis and social diseases are caus-ng the native population to diminish in the Territory.

PEYOTE—AS NARCOTIC AND CULT

Peyote (sometimes called "mescal") is a species of cactus grown in northern Mexico, the top of which when cut off and dried forms so-called "buttons," which are eaten either in their dry, brittle state or made into a tea. The Spanish padres called it *raíz diabólica* or "devil's root." Introduced into Oklahoma and other southwestern states in the nineties, it has had an alarming growth in the past decade. From the southern tribes the habit has gradually spread northward, perhaps as far as the Canadian border. The cult that has grown up around the use of this narcotic sloughs off as it moves away from its ancestral home, many of its pagan forms to take on certain ritualistic and Christian appendages, until it now poses as a "Christian" religion and its priests assume the right to administer the sacraments. Some claim authority to celebrate the marriage ceremony. Where Indians are given an outlet for emotion in religious forms that satisfy their pride in a distinctive Indian religion, peyote is not popular. This is strikingly illustrated among those tribes in Washington and Oregon who have embraced "Shakerism," a curious combination of Christian principles and superstition—not to be confused with the historic cult of Shakers in the eastern states.

Dr. Robert E. L. Newberne, former Chief Medical Supervisor of the U. S. Indian Service,[17] in commenting on the growth of this cult, says:

> The extension of the peyote religion is due to active missionary efforts on the part of those who saw in it an opportunity to gain personal leadership in promoting the tenets of a cult whose emblem of the eucharist is an intoxicant which stimulates and entrances far beyond the powers of alcohol and yet permits the retention of consciousness, thus leaving the mind free to witness, although in help-

essness, a panoramic scene of color visions that transport the soul into a paradise where it is lost in wonder, . . . or into an inferno on the wall of which in fiery characters are written the sins of the observer.

At the time of the publication of Dr. Newberne's pamphlet the use of peyote as a habit-forming drug was being definitely discouraged by the Indian Office. For the decade following, the annual appropriation bill carried an item "for the suppression of intoxicating liquors *and peyote*." [18]

With the present administration came a complete reversal of policy. At the Commissioner's request,[19] the words "and peyote" were omitted from current appropriation bills, on the ground that peyote was a sacramental substance like the bread and wine of the communion service, and that to discriminate against its use would be to oppose one denomination of the Christian church.[20]

In more recent years the subject of peyote addiction has challenged the attention of specialists in the medical field, especially psychiatrists. Dr. Moorman P. Prosser, assistant physician at the Central Oklahoma State Hospital at Norman, Oklahoma, where he is engaged upon a special study of the effects of the use of peyote, spoke on June 7, 1939, before the regional conference of the National Fellowship of Indian Workers at Bacone College in Oklahoma. In the course of his vigorous address, he emphasized the perilous nature of peyote as a drug addiction:

I feel that we are all agreed that the habitual or excessive use of any drug is harmful. The degree of harm which is done, however, depends not only upon the type of drug which is taken, but also upon the type of person who takes it. Not only will a single drug affect different persons in varying manners and degrees; a single drug will also affect the same individual differently upon varying occasions. And so it is with peyote. . . . Primarily it appears to

> affect the mind of its users, but it also impairs the normal functions of the body. The greatest havoc wreaked by the drug is the deterioration of personality, the lowering of moral standards, the impairment of social consciousness, and the loss of economic independence observed in the chronic addict. Obviously these changes harm not only the peyote user himself, but they have an injurious and degrading effect upon the community and society as a whole.
>
> Certainly the addict to peyote, like the addict to alcohol, is intoxicated, or poisoned. And who will deny that repeated intoxication is harmful to the human body, the human mind, and to society?
>
> Like alcohol, peyote offers its devotees an escape from the realities of life, but hidden in its fragrance of fantasy lie the thorns of ill health, mental deterioration, and economic failure. Like alcohol, peyote offers temporary relief from difficult and oppressive problems. Like alcohol, it solves no problem whatsoever, but merely creates more difficulties for its addict to face when the effect of the drug wears off. Moral, social, and economic standards suffer through its use, and it should be labeled "Poison—Danger—Keep Away."

In full realization of this menace, certain tribes have taken specific actions to outlaw this drug, a notable example being that of the Navajo Tribal Council, which in June, 1940, passed a strong resolution "to prevent the introduction in or the use of peyote on the Navajo Reservation." [21] The Pine Ridge Tribal Council (S. D.) passed a similar resolution about two years ago, but ratification was withheld by the Secretary of the Interior on the ground that "the ordinance infringes upon religious liberties which this Department would be vigilant to protect." [22]

Opposition to the use of peyote is strong not only among enlightened and progressive Indians; Christian missionaries have also long realized the insidious nature of this drug. Generally speaking, they have followed two methods in dealing with it: aggressive action toward prohibiting the traffic of eyote through legislative channels, including attempts to ave it classified under the Harrison Narcotic Act, and ducation. Literature prepared by experts in their fields has roved effective in interpreting the dangers of peyote addicion. At present, efforts are under way to prepare a suitable rimer for use in mission schools and young peoples' organiations. United effort on the part of all Christian agencies in ealing with this menace is an ever present challenge and will ield results of far-reaching significance.[23]

OCIAL ADJUSTMENTS

Home and community life of the Indian has been prooundly influenced by the past. The primitive home was imple as to organization; the wants were few. Everyday ife was largely determined by the nomadic habits of the ribe—here today, gone tomorrow. Or a place might become ewitched and declared taboo; hence it was high time to nove on. Moreover, the type of habitation was reflected by he Indian's mode of life and outlook. "It is a shame to cover he top of our wigwam so that the Good Ruler cannot look lown upon his children in their home life," was a saying not ncommon to some tribes.

Today the housing situation has materially changed. From he tepee, wigwam, and wickiup to the log cabin, frame dwellng, and modern bungalow marks successive steps in housng as well as a change in the way of thinking. A veteran nissionary, son of a pioneer on the great central plains, thus hronicles the change:

> The Indian wants a house with a roof that will not leak; a stove, so that the smoke of the open hearth will not drive him out of the house; springbeds to indulge his weary body, instead of the hard ground or dirt floor; a board floor to keep out the dust and damp of the ground. . . . The grandmother, when as a girl she returned

from school, removed the dishes from under the stove to a soap bo nailed onto the wall; the mother puts them in a china closet; th daughter puts them into a pantry or on the mahogany sideboard Thus we witness the transition from the old to the new.

Perhaps the most far-reaching factor in social adjustmen is the influence exerted by the mobile civilization that th Indian faces in sharp contrast to the static tribalism of a earlier day. The old isolation is gone and with it much o the old social order. The Indian, in common with uproote peoples of whatever racial background, suffers from too muc mobility—the mobility due to drought and depression, th work in various government relief projects, which necessi tates living in temporary shelters, and now the widesprea employment in war industries, which has led to the break-u of home life. All this has too often encouraged the loosenin of marital ties. Promiscuity, separations, divorces, and broke homes tend to follow. Reports from fifty-four reservations [2] indicate that so-called "Indian custom" marriages, whil showing a decline in recent years on some reservations, registe an increase on others. Especially baffling to the missionary a well as to other social workers is the fact that the Federa government, as well as certain state governments, counte-nance this practice.[25]

This problem of "Indian custom" marriages used as a cloak to cover illicit relations is by no means limited by interna-tional boundary lines. Government officials as well as mission-ary workers both in Canada and Alaska complain of the in-creasing looseness in morals and of homes broken by marital strife. In Alaska there are no adequate marriage laws and immorality is reported as flagrant.

Answering the question, "Would you favor having the Indians of your reservation come under state laws with re-spect to marriage and divorce?",[26] a great majority favor xtension of such jurisdiction, although reasons are given why a particular group may not yet be ready for this step. Here are typical answers. From Tongue River, Montana: "Not at present; state laws do very little for Indians, nor do aws of whites fit situations that arise here"; from a section of the Navajo country: "Here it would probably not be wise for some time yet. Areas too large. Much educational work yet to be done. Inadequate state control would simply result n broken laws."

The inconsistent position of the Indian citizen, partly under Federal and partly under state jurisdiction, is recognized. A discriminating statement on the subject of the state jurisdiction is the following:

I would favor this reservation [Sac and Fox, Iowa] coming under tate laws with respect to marriage and divorce provided it comes about in such a way that it can be enforced. If it is imposed upon he Indian country, enforcement will be difficult. . . . The new Council is now feeling responsibility for the moral conditions on he reservation and desires to have the help of the state laws in the narriage situation. We will do well to let them take the initiative n approaching the State Legislature in this matter that their cooperation later be safeguarded.

In this connection the National Fellowship of Indian Workers, in 1941, unanimously put itself on record as favoring state jurisdiction:

Believing in Christian citizenship for the American Indian, we recommend that all cooperating agencies devote their efforts to have enacted into law a statute defining their status. We urge that the following text be presented to the Congress of the United States for enactment into law:

"All U. S. citizens of Indian blood residing within the limits of an organized community, township, district, county, or other government unit of any state or territory of the United States, shall be

subject to all the laws, civil and criminal, of such jurisdictions i
the same measure as non-Indian citizens, provided that nothing i
this Act shall affect or impair the trust existing on Indian-owne
land and tribal property."

THE USE OF ALCOHOL

History records that to the Dutch colonists falls the un
enviable distinction of opening the first rum barrels in th
Indian country. Rum was soon a prime element in barte
the Indian too often exchanging all his goods for fire wate

The menace of this fire water has by no means lessene
since the passing of the fur trader. All closely connecte
with present-day Indian life and affairs seem agreed tha
liquor stands as the most urgent problem. Among contribut
ing factors are:

1. Repeal of the Eighteenth Amendment. Although reser
vation Indians are presumably subject to prohibition edict
formulated from time to time, they are caught up in th
resurgence of liquor consumption so prevalent among thei
fellow-citizens of white ancestry. "If we could just refor
a few white folk the Indians would get along pretty well,
is the way one worker expresses it.

2. Ease of procurement. "Indians are drinking far mor
than during the days of the Eighteenth Amendment becaus
it was somewhat harder to get at that time. They have littl
trouble securing drink today," is a sentiment reflected b
many in the field.

3. Confusion regarding liquor laws. A reservation worke
of long experience states the case thus: "The governmen
legalizes the curse, then ties the hands of the agents, an
arrests the Indian for drinking it." Often a reservation i
considered a sort of "no man's land" from the angle of la
enforcement by state as well as Federal authorities.

4. The easy-come-easy-go money of those engaged in de-ense industries. "It is a major problem every pay day," is he all too frequent comment of field workers; "Worse when ddicts have money," is another. This situation is by no neans limited to Indians, however. That many social and ealth problems are due to liquor is the well-nigh universal estimony. Says a Pima Indian worker: "Liquor is the biggest indrance to our progress. Many broken homes, deaths (acci-ental) of our young people, and health problems are due o the use of liquor." And another concludes, "If we did not ave the liquor and peyote curses, our missionary work would e an entirely different story."

High government officials are evidently not unmindful of his menace. A former Commissioner of Indian Affairs, ad-ressing a group of welfare workers at a Lake Mohonk con-erence, said: "If we can save the American Indian from the urse of whiskey, we can save him from pretty much all the ther evils that threaten him."

Speaking of problems related to law enforcement, the resent Commissioner of Indian Affairs stated in his annual eport for 1938: "Most of the serious crimes committed by ndians have intoxicating liquor as a contributing cause." he Secretary of the Interior says that this situation "presents ne of the most baffling problems in connection with the uardianship of Indians and one of the greatest problems in ndian life."

Commenting on the same question, the late Secretary of he Indian Rights Association, Matthew K. Sniffen, says:

> It should be noted that the Indian area is very extensive; that the iquor Suppression personnel is far too small to cover the field dequately, and that the appropriation granted by Congress for this ork is wholly inadequate. These facts can be urged by official urces as an excuse for not checking the evil.

But it should not be overlooked that the departmental regulatio now in force specify that "superintendents are primarily responsib for the enforcement of the liquor laws, as far as pertains to t reservations and the Indians under their jurisdiction."

These regulations prohibit the introduction of liquor on Indi reservations by anyone—Indian or white. . . . The final senten of the Office regulations states, "Officers or employees who viola these laws or this rule render themselves subject to dismissal fro the Service and prosecution in the courts." [27]

Nor have the Canadian Indians and natives of Alaska bee spared the ravages of the liquor traffic. It has been said [28] th from 1828 to 1858 the Hudson's Bay Company had refuse to sell liquor to the Indians and had proved a stabilizing fa tor in their social life. But following the gold rush in t early sixties, and again in the late nineties, the flow of fi water was free and full, with but slight interruptions. Whi the Dominion government has enacted fairly stringent la against the introduction of liquor into the reserves, neverth less not only native intoxicants are being used but, accordin to responsible officials in church and state, considerable qua tities of ardent spirits are being consumed by present-da Indians, especially when off the reserves.

In Alaska the liquor situation is alarming and has been growing menace since repeal. A missionary who has spe seven years in that country does not hesitate to state th "the Indians of Alaska are dying out due to liquor and di ease." Describing conditions where he was formerly statione he says: "The greatest obstacle to Christian work is liquo There are over fifty saloons and liquor stores in our city of little over four thousand people. Almost ten dollars per pe son per month is spent here for liquor. The hold this ev has on many natives and whites is one that can be broke only by the power of God and through Christian teaching."

From time to time a limited number of tribes have inserted in their law and order codes certain regulations with respect to the liquor traffic, but with indifferent results. This despite the fact that the Indian Department employs "62 Indian judges, 60 Indian chiefs of police, and 135 Indian police with the staff of 25 special and deputy special officers" for purposes of law enforcement.[30]

With respect to the Federal liquor laws, a number being of many years standing, a publication [31] issued under the auspices of a well known temperance agency contributes the following: "Many protests have urged modification of the present Federal liquor statute on the grounds of discrimination and a stigma of inferiority." Should any such change offer a substantial lessening of the curse, then surely all should join in bringing about legislation toward that desired end. But is it simply a matter of legislation? Have we not always assumed in our dealings with the red man that another law or two will solve all his difficulties?

The Christian standard is that human relations are a much deeper matter than law; that the kingdom to be conquered, the battle to be fought, is in the mind and heart of man. In short, human nature must be changed. Said a student of the Cheyenne tribe at a summer conference: "Peyote and whiskey are the worst habits my people have. Only God can help us overcome that. I am going to pray and work to down these evils." Surely, "it is the glory of the Christian religion not to be set apart from life, but to permeate it powerfully." [32]

SOCIAL AND RECREATIONAL OUTLETS

Undoubtedly the peyote cult and the use of liquor, as well as the Indian ceremonial dance as usually indulged in, cater to those seeking pleasurable means of filling their leisure. For the Indians, in common with human kind, enjoy social relationships. The question is not whether they will get together but where and how.

In the recent study of fifty-four typical reservations already referred to, it was found that the economic, social, and moral by-products of Indian dances were generally considered grave. As summing up some of the effects of these dances, ceremonial and otherwise, the following from the Navajo field is significant:

> Some of the worshippers of Indian culture speak of the devoutness of the Indian in his ceremonial dance. Too often the worshipper sees only that the Indian is seeking after God, not realizing how far astray he has sought or how far short he has come in finding that soul satisfaction that comes with the love of a personal God and a Saviour of men who has shown to all the world the greatness of service to others. And not all the Navajo dances are devil chasers or prayers for rain. The squaw dance is said by the Navajos themselves to be nothing more than prostitution at public auction. I asked a superintendent of a government school how he accounted for the fact that the government work program had brought about a decrease in the number of girls attending school as well as the number of boys when only the boys were employed. He laughed and said that the girls went to the squaw dances and got most of the boys' money. This tangent only leads back to the idea of a high moral standard among the Navajos. The tribe is made up of individuals who differ in their tastes, talents, and standards of living as widely as do those of the white race. Many of the Navajos do have high standards of morality and are sincere in their worship.[33]

In western Canada and the Pacific Northwest, the social evils of the *potlatch* (described in Chapter Two) have long been recognized. A Canadian writer expressed the situation in the following language:

> While a *potlatch* was a gathering together of many tribes in a social way, the attendant evils far outweighed any possible good. The givers went any length to obtain coveted power; even the honor

of wives and daughters was bartered to provide money for the expenses of the *potlatch,* which left a trail of debt, poverty, and suffering. It was debasing morally, retarded education, perpetuated pagan customs and ideals, and was a hindrance to economic progress.[34]

It is obvious to those cognizant of Indian affairs on both sides of the international boundary line that the recreational element of the average Indian ceremonial, whether commercialized or not, offers a compelling appeal. The powwow under whatever designation or auspices becomes a gathering place where youth meets youth, age meets age, acquaintances are renewed, talk-fests are indulged in, and Indian characteristic hospitality holds sway. What an educational opportunity for Christian agencies to demonstrate that proper recreation, games, dramatization, and creative art answer human needs for creative activity and social contacts and have a rightful place in building wholesome community life!

REFERENCES

1. *Mère Marie of the Ursulines,* by Agnes Repplier, p. 60. New York, Literary Guild, 1931.
2. *Natural History,* by Dr. Clark Wissler, as quoted in *The Literary Digest,* September 15, 1934, p. 17.
3. See discussion of land tenure, Chap. III, pp. 50 ff.
4. According to the Statistical Supplement to the *Annual Report of the Commissioner of Indian Affairs* for the fiscal year ending June 30, 1940, Indians are credited with total land holdings of 55,406,412 acres, of which 17,573,936 are held as trust allotted, 36,046,660 tribal, and 1,785,816 "government owned," that is, presumably the title is in the name of the United States "for use of Indians." Table VIII—Lands under the jurisdiction of the Office of Indian Affairs.
5. See "The Indian's Master Problem: Land," in *Indians at Work,* October 1, 1933, p. 4.
6. *Annual Report of the Commissioner of Indian Affairs* for 1924.

7. According to the Annual Report of the Revolving Credit Fund for the fiscal year ending June 30, 1942, appropriations of $5,424,600 had been made from 1936-1942; of this amount $861,200 was authorized for administration, leaving $4,563,400 available for loans. Pamphlet No. 8, Division of Extension and Industry, November 1, 1942, p. 4.
8. Report of Secretary of the Interior to Advisory Council of One Hundred, Washington, D. C., December 12, 1923.
9. From Statistical Supplement, *op. cit.*, Table XIII.
10. From an address delivered at Farmington, N. M., June 13, 1941.
11. *Indians in Urban Life*, a survey of families residing in a typical midwestern city (1937). On file in the University of Wisconsin Library, Madison.
12. At Caughnawaga, a Mohawk village southwest of Montreal (pop. 2,200), there is an industrialized group of part-blood Indians, many of whom are engaged in the structural steel industry in United States as well as Canadian cities, and find ready employment at good wages.
13. *The Changing Indian*, edited by Oliver La Farge, chapter on "Indian Health—Past, Present and Future," by J. G. Townsend, p. 30. Norman, University of Oklahoma Press, 1942.
14. A discussion of medical missions is found in Chap. VI, pp. 122 ff.
15. La Farge, *op. cit.*, p. 32.
16. Pub. 645, 77th Cong. H. R. 6845.
17. *Peyote*, an abridged compilation from the files of the Bureau of Indian Affairs, by Dr. Robert E. L. Newberne, p. 19. Washington, D. C., 1923.
18. In the Act approved January 24, 1923, making appropriations for the Interior Department for the year beginning July 1, 1923, is a clause: "For the suppression of the traffic in intoxicating liquors and deleterious drugs, *including peyote*, among Indians, $25,000."
19. See Hearings on Interior Department Appropriation Bill for 1936, p. 690.
20. "The Native American Church" for the practice of the peyote sacrament, was incorporated at El Reno, Oklahoma, October 10, 1918. The act of incorporation was "revised" on April 24, 1934, by amendment whereby the peyote cult became "the religion of our forefathers."

1. Resolution No. C. J. 40 by Navajo Tribal Council, June 3 1940, signed by J. C. Morgan, chairman.
2. Office Letter of October 14, 1943, No. 29839-43.
3. For further study of peyote, see "What About Peyote?" issued by the Home Missions Council of North America, New York, 1941, and prepared by a sub-committee of that organization; also "Peyote Intoxication—Some Psychological Aspects of the Peyote Rite," by Drs. Bromberg and Tranter in *The Journal of Nervous and Mental Disease*, May, 1943, p. 518; the latter, together with "Some Pertinent Comments," by Philip M. Riley, are available in leaflet form at the Home Missions Council, 297 Fourth Avenue, New York 10, N. Y.
4. "Current Social Conditions in Indian Life," compiled from reports from fifty-four typical reservations, 1939-40.
5. Circular No. M-25563, Dept. of the Interior, Office of the Solicitor, April 12, 1930; also Circular issued November 9, 1934, by the Commissioner of Indian Affairs and approved by the Acting Secretary of the Interior, already referred to in Chap. III, p. 66.
6. Report from fifty-four reservations, cited above.
7. From an address delivered at the Regional Conference of Indian Workers at Farmington, N. M., June, 1938.
8. *One Hundred Years of Canadian Methodist Missions*, by Mrs. Frederick C. Stephenson, pp. 158-159. Toronto, Young People's Forward Movement, 1925.
9. The Rev. Donald G. Christiansen, former missionary under the Presbyterian Church in the U. S. A.
10. *Drink and the Indians*, p. 6. Washington, D. C., Board of Temperance of the Methodist Church, 1939.
11. *Ibid.*, p. 6.
12. *Rational Living*, by Henry Churchill King, p. 18. New York, The Macmillan Co., 1916.
13. *Ganado News Bulletin*, Ganado, Arizona, June, 1936.
14. Stephenson, *op. cit.*, pp. 222-223.

Chapter V

EDUCATIONAL DEVELOPMENTS AND TRENDS

by John H. Holst

THE DARING EXPLORERS OF THE NEW WORLD WERE followed closely by devoted missionaries who gave their lives in carrying out the divine injunction to take the gospel to all mankind. The Indians of North America offered an inviting field for the spiritual harvest, but the pioneer settlers, as they pushed back the wilderness frontiers, so often disregarded Christian principles in dealing with the Indians that a powerful counteracting force to that of the Christian teachers was exerted. Nevertheless, it can be said that up to 1850 the only educational privileges provided for the Indians were those made available by the missionaries. Every early religious mission set up some form of teaching agency.

The mission school carried forward the education of the Indian at a time when there was no widespread public support for such an enterprise. In reality, the United States Indian Service developed out of the zeal of church missionary societies. Their efforts on behalf of Indian welfare were first recognized by the Federal government about 1820, when it began an annual appropriation of ten thousand dollars for Indian education. As a result of missionary efforts from old colonial days on through the early Federal period, such progress had been made that when the time came for government schools to be established they were able in many tribes to deal with a fairly advanced type of Indian pupil. Strong missionary influence enabled mission schools long to hold their own in competition with government gratuity.

The mission schools were founded primarily to teach the Indians the Christian way of life; at the same time they gave, in most instances, careful attention to the adaptation of Indian youth to their social and economic environment. The Christian idealism of the schools softened and gave tone to their practical utilitarianism. They were really developing communities to which each Indian scholar contributed his part and assumed responsibility. Support was usually so limited and so precarious that each institution was thrown mainly upon its own local resources. Individual initiative and careful planning from day to day was the rule enforced by necessity.

The schools varied widely but certain features were common to all: the religious instruction and the constant effort by the missionaries to apply their teaching to the circumstances surrounding the lives of their pupils. Of course, the Indians were to have homes and were to be self-supporting; therefore, most of the mission schools acquired land that served a double purpose—that of contributing to the support of the school and that of furnishing practical opportunities for the children to learn how to maintain themselves on the land. Buildings and equipment, while usually inadequate, furnished an incentive to continual progress. The school might not have a farm and shops, but it would have a garden and rooms for industrial instruction, as well as a place for the actual production of necessary food and clothing.

INFLUENCE OF MISSION SCHOOLS

From the days of the "Indian Charity School" at Lebanon, Connecticut (later moved to Hanover, New Hampshire, and rechristened Dartmouth College), down to the immediate present, the contribution of the mission schools to Indian life and thought looms large. Perhaps no other single factor has been more determinative in disseminating Christian teaching, in raising the standard of morals, and in producing a trained leadership. When in 1896 Congress ceased to make direct appropriations for the maintenance of mission schools, the number of Protestant institutions diminished. However, this was not altogether due to sporadic policies and financial retrenchment. An appreciable number of church missionary agencies felt that however admirable the *esprit de corps* and personnel, the atmosphere and environment, of such institutions might be, the Indian children would be better off if not segregated.

Typical of a mission school's response to a definite need in a critical transition period of a tribe is the record of one established among the Jicarilla Apaches in New Mexico several decades ago. The outstanding fact in the lives of these people at the time was disease. Seventy per cent were afflicted with tuberculosis. This scourge contributed to their poverty, caused their numbers to dwindle, and prevented them from securing proper education even for the healthy children. Health became a primary concern for both church and government agencies on the reservation. A mutual working agreement was decided on whereby the Reformed Church mission took over the responsibility for educating the healthy children, while the government converted an old boarding school into a sanatorium—which later became a well staffed institution—where children predisposed to tuberculosis were taught and given a chance at robust health. This was in 1920. A new mission boarding school was opened at once. A fine spirit of cooperation between government and missionary agencies was thus developed. Since the reservation is a mountainous country, the roads not always passable, and the Indian homes widely scattered, the mission school filled a long-felt need. In time, as health conditions improved, the church provided a dormitory home for approximately one hundred children while the government assumed responsibility for their secular education. At a still later stage, one finds the mission developing community work, through the splendid facilities of a social center, as well as reaching out to the more isolated parts of the reservation through the use of a well equipped "gospel trailer." Today the mission school as such no longer exists, but the spirit engendered in the hearts and minds of the Jicarilla Apache youth lives on.

OFF-THE-RESERVATION EDUCATION

Early Indian education was necessarily in boarding schools. The semi-nomadic nature of many tribes and the home conditions that generally prevailed made training in a stable environment the obvious course. But for the most part these schools were located within the areas occupied by the respective tribes and were known as "reservation" schools. It was Captain (later General) R. H. Pratt, an army officer in charge of a group of Indian prisoners, who developed the plan for shifting the base of education away from reservation life to centers where contact with civilization would teach the red man a different way of living. First by his teaching adult persons at Fort Marion, Florida, then by sending to Hampton Institute in Virginia those who had shown an eagerness for more training, and finally by establishing at old Fort Carlisle in Pennsylvania a school for Indian youth, he translated into action his belief, vigorously and often expressed:

"To civilize the Indian, put him in the midst of civilization. To keep him civilized, keep him there."

Carlisle Indian School, founded in 1879, put a new impetus into Indian education. The zeal and devotion of its founder were imparted to pupils and teachers alike. The quarter century of Pratt's service to Indian education was a landmark.

The success of Carlisle led to the establishment of other "non-reservation" boarding schools—Haskell Institute in Lawrence, Kansas, Sherman Institute in Riverside, California, Chemawa School near Salem, Oregon, and others. None, however, was so distant from Indian country as Carlisle, and in none were there leaders with the ardor and individuality of Captain Pratt. For a generation or more these schools gave needed training, physical and mental, to Indian youth, eventually raising the standards of training until they approximated those of a manual high school.

The non-reservation boarding school in its general features followed the pattern of the better mission schools. There was usually a school farm, garden, and dairy, which, together with the operation and maintenance of the school plant, occupied most of the time and attention of the employees and pupils alike. The course of study attempted to correlate learning with farm upkeep and production. Every hour of the day for seven days a week was exactly scheduled for both employees and pupils.

As the non-reservation schools grew in buildings, staff, and equipment, the Indian Bureau based the support of any particular school on the number of children in attendance. Hence the schools sent out recruiting agents to bring in more and more pupils to increase their attendance quota. Schools encroached on the territory of each other, and agents from two or more schools might clash in territory far from the schools represented by any one of them. Thus, thousands of

Indian children who could have been accommodated better in public schools or mission schools near their homes were brought to the boarding schools.

THE "OUTING" SYSTEM

Under Captain Pratt, the Carlisle Indian School began the "outing" system in 1880, sending out sixteen pupils for summer placement with rural families. The placements increased until they numbered several hundreds each year. Usually there were twice as many boys as girls on outing. Most of them were placed with white families in the near-by counties of Pennsylvania, but others were sent to neighboring states. The Indian pupils liked the system. The white families with whom they were placed treated them as their own children. A contemporary report states: "These young Indians are brought into the most vital relationship with the highest type of American rural life. They acquire the habits of neatness, industry, thrift, and self-reliance. They acquire a good working knowledge of English and a practical acquaintance with all kinds of domestic and farm work. They associate with the farmer's children, eat at the same table with them, attend the same church and Sunday school, and for four months of each year, attend the same day school. A better scheme for converting them into intelligent, honest, American citizens, self-respectful and self-helpful, could scarcely be devised."[1]

No other Indian school used the outing system so effectively for the enrichment of its educational program as did Carlisle, but a similar system was later used in certain centers where Indian ex-students were accustomed to assemble.

One of the most noted and successful of these outing centers was conducted at Los Angeles for several years before and after 1930 by Mrs. Frances D. Hall, widow of Indian

Superintendent Harwood Hall. At that time the Indian population of Los Angeles numbered many hundreds.

The more daring, ambitious, and restless among the younger Indians sooner or later heard the glamorous stories of life in this mecca of aspiring artists and movie stars. Many of them ultimately found their way to the "Gay Carcassonne" of their dreams. Whether the city should become for them a consuming fire or a refiner's flame depended upon the provision for their protection, organization, and direction.

The Indian Office was fortunate in being able to initiate there one of the most significant Indian welfare services in the life of Indian girls. Much of this was due to the field matron, Mrs. Hall, who had an insight into Indian life, a sympathy with Indians in their struggles and aspirations, and a lively faith in their ultimate success.

The story of the Los Angeles outing center is an interesting chapter in Indian education. Hundreds of girls were annually placed in employment or in school, or in both. Some of the larger boarding schools sent girls to Mrs. Hall; many older girls drifted to the center, the whole aim of which was to educate and train Indian girls to insure them the greatest possible opportunities for success in life. They were placed in homes that typified the higher American ideals; they had the status of members of the families with whom they lived; they had opportunities for a satisfying social life; and, so far as possible, the opportunity to select work along the lines of their preferred vocations. Hundreds of them attended public school.

THE INDIAN AND THE PUBLIC SCHOOL

Within a dozen years after the founding of Carlisle, there began a movement aimed at placing Indian children in the public schools. Many tribes were ready for this; others had not reached a stage where such adjustment was possible. A great number of Indian children were so placed in the last decade of the century, and reaped the great advantage of constant contact on equal terms with their white contemporaries.

Since that time there have been successive waves of policy, to and from public schools. Successive administrations have stressed boarding schools—both reservation and non-reservation; or Indian day schools; or public schools, as the head of the service directed. With reference to day schools, not heretofore described in this study, it should be noted that they were patterned at first after the mission schools. In place of industrial classes as conducted in the ordinary boarding school, the program provides for work in school gardens and simple home crafts.

There have been three or more periods of emphasis upon the public school, and today, in spite of the current tendency to draw Indians back into more complete dependence upon the Federal government, it is probable that at least half of the children of Indian blood are going to local schools with their white neighbors.

It has been amply demonstrated that where the Indians are surrounded by a white population sufficient to make this school experience a real mingling of the races, a great improvement in Indian-white relations has followed. For a normal relationship between the children in the schools has tended to normalize the communication between adults. This, in turn, points the way to the goal of racial harmony and understanding that is implicit in the Christian goal for community life.

Typical of such schools is the Union Graded School, located in a rural section of Adair County, Oklahoma. Of the 450 pupils enrolled fully one-third are Indians, giving it probably the largest enrollment of Indian children in any public school in the state. At least 90 pupils are in the high school department, where two years in home economics and general agricultural subjects are scheduled. The children, regardless of racial background, mingle freely in classroom and playground, participate in athletics and musical organizations, and share the same opportunities for weekday religious instruction offered by the visiting missionary—who, by the way, is a general favorite with teachers and pupils alike. This is but one example of the mingling of the races made possible in the institution that every American so highly prizes—the common school.

Though there has been an increasing number of Indian children in public schools ever since there has been a public school system, the first tuition contract for the education of Indian children in a public school was made in 1891 with a district in California. The number of Indian children under Federal tuition increased rapidly from 1914 to 1930, when there were 34,915, not including a very large number of Indian children who were enrolled through other channels. By that year the total appropriation for this purpose amounted to $750,000.

About 1929 the Office of Indian Affairs began to contribute to the building of public grade and high schools attended by Indians. The results were disappointing. In the first place, the combination of local and Federal funds produced buildings beyond the ability of the community to support, since future maintenance was not taken into account. In the second place, the cooperatively constructed buildings more often went to those towns having a strong "Chamber of Commerce" spirit rather than where the need was greatest. In the third place, the clamor for Federal funds for public school buildings began to have a political bearing.

Along with the movement for Federal cooperation in pub-
ic school building, the Indian Office undertook a new venture
—that of building in Indian communities Federal day schools
t which whites rather than Indians should pay tuition.
Turtle Mountain, North Dakota, Pine Ridge, South Dakota,
nd Standing Rock, with Fort Yates, in North Dakota, as
he center, are examples. The result was elaborate and costly
chool plants far beyond the needs of the communities. The
xperience at Turtle Mountain is worth noting. On this
ittle reservation lived an impoverished people. Their lands
nd possible industries were insufficient both in quantity and
quality to sustain a fifth of the residents. The reservation was
lready supplied with a dozen public schools that were more
dequately serving the educational needs of the people than
as the new system ever been able to serve them. There were
o non-Indians to attend the new school except a few em-
loyees' children, and they went to more distant public
chools. Yet, at Turtle Mountain, the Indian Office built a
nodern school plant extensive enough to accommodate all,
ven after the Office, through its relief administration, had
nore than doubled the resident Indian population. Here were
modern school, hospital, employees' building, and many
esidences, all within plain view of a mission school that had
ormerly supplemented the public schools and that, despite
Federal antagonism and competition, continued to serve the
ducational needs of the Indians.

Over forty miles of improved roads were constructed at a
cost of more than a quarter of a million dollars for the seven
great school buses to use. The whole construction program
cost well over $500,000, and that in a community unable
to support a tenth of that amount if ever called upon to do
so. The public schools were then closed, except one in a far
corner of the reservation, which remained open until the end

of the first year with an average attendance of ninety-tw per cent of the enrollment, while the great new school wit its seven big buses to carry the children from home to schoc and back, with its hot noon meal, and with its progressiv program of education and numerous employees, had an aver age attendance of only sixty-three per cent.

CONSOLIDATION AND THE DAY SCHOOL

In recent years public school consolidation in progressiv rural areas in many states has become an accepted means fo enlarging the educational community around a central schoc plant. Transportation is used to bring the children from out lying areas. In line with these changing practices, the India Office decided to adopt consolidation and to provide mean of transportation to Indian day schools. Many serious an expensive mistakes were made. Much of the Indian countr was sparsely settled and groups were widely scattered an separated by long distances. The windswept plains of th Sioux with their winter blizzards; the barren uplands of th Navajos with their shifting population; and the hot desert of the Papagos and Pimas, were not adapted to the rural con solidated school. Yet in these areas, especially in the South west, the outlying schools were abandoned in favor of highl developed central plants. This necessitated the constructio of expensive roads. These were slow in building and difficul of upkeep. In very many instances it was found later that th central plants had not been properly located with referenc to the communities to be served. Because of the cost the could not reasonably be changed or abandoned. One exampl among many that could be given may serve to illustrate som of the adverse results of Indian school consolidation as it wa attempted:

The great Papago reservation lying along the Mexican border has no thickly settled rural areas. Here, under consolidation, the school population was shifted from far circumference to center and back again every twenty-four hours. One bus route was seventy-two miles in round-trip length and over roads so nearly impassable that children spent more time on the buses than in the school and had few daylight hours at home. This condition prevailed to a less degree on the Pima reservation bordering the Papago on the north, and on the great Navajo reservation.

It is true that not many public schools were available to the Papagos and Pimas, but local day schools and excellent mission schools had been serving them in a very effective way. Now that the consolidated day school with its arduous transportation has so signally failed in this arid Southwest area, the Indians are turning again to the mission schools in increasing numbers. On the Pima reservation, especially, the mission school attendance is greater than at the Federal day schools. It is testimony to the value of the teaching missions when the Indians turn again to them after a long compulsory trial of an elaborate gratuity system of day schools. In this connection it is of interest to note that the Presbyterians have two mission schools serving this area. One, known as the Tucson Indian Training School, was the first Protestant school to be established for Indians in Arizona, and has an enrollment of one hundred and sixty boys and girls of the elementary and high school level; another is San Miguel on the Papago reservation, where community work centers around the mission day school. A number of Roman Catholic mission schools also serve this region, notably St. John's Boarding School at Gila Crossing, San Xavier, originally established in 1864, and eight to ten day schools, a majority being on the Papago reservation.

"PROGRESSIVE" EDUCATION

By 1930 the course of study in Indian schools had been developed to the standards of the American public school system. But in that year the theories of so-called "progressive" education were introduced, and the idea was developed that the tastes and environment of the child should determine his training. The three R's were relegated to the rear while Indian arts, legends, and traditions were fostered. The use of the Indian's own language instead of English was represented as a feature of the "self-expression" toward which the system was directed, and this trend would have been pushed farther had it not been that the teacher seldom, if ever, could tell what the pupils were expressing in the Tewa or Paiute or Apache tongue.

At the same time there was a movement to extend the use of public schools, but in such a way as to defeat one of the chief purposes of public school attendance. For by insisting upon Federal payment of tuition for Indian pupils—ostensibly in lieu of non-taxation of Indian lands, even in many cases where these pupils had always been accepted without charge—the emphasis was laid upon segregation instead of integration. The child was thus set aside from his playmates on the ground of Indian ancestry. Many boarding schools and some day schools were closed. A supervisor of public school relations was appointed and a field staff built up to expedite the program of transfer. Arrangements were made with several states, notably California, Washington, and Minnesota, to take over the Indian education work within their respective boundaries.

Indian education under its present direction has devoted itself mainly to the development of the unit dormitory in the remaining boarding schools, and to the building up of Indian day schools in preference to the transfer of Indian children to public schools; hence, the Federal day school has definitely come into competition with the public school. As an example there may be cited the case of the Sac and Fox Indians at Tama, Iowa. Near these Indians are excellent public schools that could have been opened to them without difficulty. The Indians did not want a day school, but the Office insisted on building for them a completely equipped community school far larger than the little community will ever need or be able to use, much less support. It merely serves to check their progress and to hold them in perpetual wardship.

Stockbridge, in Wisconsin, furnishes another illustration. The Mohicans there had been assimilated, but they were regathered on newly purchased submarginal land where they have no choice but to live dependent on charity. They came out of the larger community of which they had been a component part and whose established institutions they had been sharing equally with their white neighbors and unintentionally re-entered into Federal wardship. A magnificent community school was built for them from gratuity funds and must continually be so supported, yet public elementary and high schools were then, and still are, just as conveniently located for them as this charity school.

BLIGHT OF DEPENDENCY

The educational situation on the former Flathead reservation in Montana illustrates the difficulty of community building where Indians, now almost completely assimilated, live scattered among their white brothers but do not have the obligation or the privilege of making their contribution to the common life on an equality with other citizens. In consequence, both Indians and non-Indians suffer. Here the remnants of several tribes and bands live scattered among a much larger population of non-Indians, while the Federal government holds in trust for them, tax exempt, fifty-four per cent of all the land of the county. Although the Indians live in peace with their white neighbors, go to school with them, marry with them, and enjoy the privileges of the best local government that can be supported by the taxpaying half of the citizenship, still the peculiar position in which the Indians find themselves leads to a deplorable situation. The Indians, through being given what is intended as a preferred status, really suffer most, because they are not only denied the better community that would be possible if they contributed their share to the cost of local government, but also the satisfaction of assumed responsibility and the pleasures of sharing in the creation of a richer community life. Is not the solution, then, the withdrawal of Federal trust over Indian property and their release from a status that tends to destroy all the finer qualities of citizenship?

Indians, like people of other races, do not value that which comes to them unsought and undesired. Men achieve because they wish for something and put forth effort to attain it. The first step in education must be to arouse interest and appreciation of education. Institutions bestowed by an outside agency, far beyond the needs or appreciation of a community, not only fail to develop the youth of the community, but actually tend to sap morale and inhibit achievement.

PRESENT TRENDS AND UNDERTAKINGS

The survey of the Indian Office [2] and its field relations in 1927 followed a barrage of attacks on the government's handling of Indian affairs by more or less informed free-lance writers. These charges were directed mainly against the educational division. Some of the attacks were prompted by the then existing conditions; but, for the most part, they overemphasized minor items out of context and thus clouded the real issues. All of this strengthened the tendency to build up and perpetuate the machinery of the Bureau through elaborate systems and plants that became vested interests of local communities, field agencies, and the Indian Office itself, and to continue long after these agencies and institutions are no longer needed to serve their original purposes. It was not that the Office needed better methods of development and operation, but rather that it needed gradually to eliminate or transfer activities and functions assumed before the general social and economic advance of the country had made it possible for the problems of the Indian to be integrated into the civic wholeness of the nation. This required a simplification of Indian Office organization and a gradual transfer of its funds and responsibilities to such general agencies of the government as would include Indians on an equal basis with other citizens.

Beginning in 1930, the Indian Office underwent a complete reorganization based on a separation of human rights from property rights. The education division, which had been the especial target of the Indian Office critics, planned a new educational program that had for its major goals: (1) elimination of Indian boarding schools as rapidly as adjustments could be made; (2) transfer of Indian children to public schools when that could be done to their advantage; (3) negotiation of contracts with individual states to take over Indian education and welfare; (4) development and extension of the Indian day school system so that, in conjunction with the public schools, it might replace boarding schools; (5) erection of modern school plants wherever needed for the new educational program; (6) provision for the care of underprivileged Indian children in private families; (7) expansion of the supervisory staff to conduct research in Indian education.

The new program started auspiciously. In connection with the extension of the Indian day schools, as we have seen, a vast construction program was begun and carried to conclusion in many expensive plants scattered over the Indian country. The system did not meet the Indian needs and is now far on the way toward decline.

A notable instance is the case of the thirty or more expensive day schools established throughout the Navajo country. The requirements of sheep herding make the Navajo family semi-nomadic, as the range of the herd must vary with the seasons. Proximity to pasture is a more immediate necessity than proximity to a school building. Further, the vast distances of the Navajo reservation are traversed by roads of the most sketchy character. For these reasons, and because the Navajo did not welcome the type of education that consisted of miniature *hogan* building and amateur weaving, both of which the child learned at home from a skilled practitioner, attendance at the day schools dwindled. When the current gasoline shortage added still further to the difficulties of the school buses that purported to supply the schools with pupils, there was a reversion to a semi-boarding school type with the pupils lodged in a "glorified" *hogan* on the school site.

Under these latest plans for Indian education, a greatly enlarged staff of experts and specialists—psychologists, anthropologists, economists, sociologists, and others—undertook special studies, each in his particular field. Thus far their recommendations have stressed the need for textbooks especially adapted to the teaching of Indian children in Indian schools.

EDUCATION IN ALASKA

Education of the natives of the Territory of Alaska was under the United States Office of Education until a few years ago, when it was transferred to the Office of Indian Affairs. It had its beginnings in missionary efforts that have supplemented Territorial and Federal agencies all along the way. The Indian Office operates a system of day schools and three vocational boarding schools, all of which, because of distance and isolation, have a maximum of local self-determination. The Territory maintains a system of Territorial public schools that is continually being extended as funds and facilities can be provided, so that now there are more natives in the Territorial public schools than in the Federal schools.

The reindeer industry and salmon fishing are the chief industries of the native Alaskans. Under the supervision of the Department of the Interior, there are thirty-nine reindeer stations. Much of the salmon fishing is carried on by natives on credit furnished by the Federal government and under its supervision. Many native communities have their own cooperative stores, credit facilities and supervision being furnished by the Federal government. The education required by the natives centers around the operation of these stores and industries. Teachers with special aptitude for such work act as local reindeer superintendents at the various reindeer stations, and local teachers assist and counsel in the management of the cooperative stores. In most of the native villages the teachers in the local schools have charge of all the activities sponsored by the Indian Office.

FUTURE FULL OF CHALLENGE

Certainly we are now approaching the final phase in the transitional period of Indian education. Many ideas and plans for it have failed, at least in part, while others have succeeded even beyond expectation. There are now from 35,000 to 50,000 Indian children in public schools, many hundreds in colleges, and the missions are still caring for as great a number as ever of the underprivileged children and those from Christian Indian homes who prefer to entrust the training of their children to the agencies of the churches.

The future is full of challenge. There is inspiring work to be done in completing the transition of Indian education and welfare to the states and to the public schools and in encouraging the Indians to complete their entry into full citizenship and to gain new understanding of the Christian life. In this, the missions will continue, not only to carry the burden of responsibility for the isolated and neglected remnants of the tribes, but also to raise the standard of Christian living among the people of the old Indian country where the Indians are turning again to their first constant friends.

REFERENCES

1. Report of Captain R. H. Pratt, Superintendent of Carlisle Indian School, to the Commissioner of Indian Affairs, November 2, 1890.
2. The report of this survey was published in 1928 under the title of *The Problem of Indian Administration*, by Lewis Merriam and others. Baltimore, Johns Hopkins Press, 1928.

Chapter VI

NEW LIFE ON NEW TRAILS:
The Christian Contribution to Indian Life

ON THE SEAL OF THE MASSACHUSETTS BAY COLONY there is engraved the figure of an Indian standing on the New England shore in an attitude of wait-ng, saying, "Come over and help us." On the seal of the ociety for Propagating the Gospel among the Indians and)thers in North America[1] there is engraved a cup that may ery well represent "the cup of salvation." Inscribed on that econd seal are the immortal words of *Zechariah* 4:6, "Not by iight nor power but by my Spirit." These two are symbolic f the Christian missionary enterprise in all ages and among ll races—first, the cry of a great need, a need real and vital, nd, second, the ability to meet that need. Thus our Lord's ommission, "Go and make disciples of all nations,"[2] is ased on two fundamental principles: first, that the message adapted to all races and all sorts of men living under vary-ıg conditions; second, that all races are endowed with the apacity to appropriate the message.

The page in the annals of the Christian church that records 's long and fruitful mission among our first Americans is singularly bright one. True, the representatives of the Cross ame to propagate a faith new and strange to the Indian eople, much of which raised hard questions in minds unused) thinking in the kind of religious terms the white man

used. "Was it not strange that the white man's God could b
in Massachusetts and in England across the sea all at one an
the same time? The great Manitou of the Indians could onl
be at one place at a time." Then, too, "God was so used t
hearing the English pray that he could very well understan
them; but was it likely that he was acquainted with th
Indian language?"

But with the message came the messenger who represente
peace rather than war, who came "to love, not to fight; t
win, not to force; to prepare the ground, to sow the goo
seed; and then, with infinite patience to wait until the see
grew and, in God's good time, brought forth fruit." Ther
are many Indians today who will gladly testify that the bes
gift received with the advent of the white man was th
gospel of Jesus Christ, a gift that they know from experi
ence does not perish with the taking.

But was not Christianity forced on these unsuspectin
natives? Did not the state dominate the church, and wher
ever the flag of the invader was planted, and the land take
possession of "in the name of the most gracious sovereign,
were not the natives called upon to confess "the faith"
The latter may have a basis in fact, at least in a few isolate
cases. One finds also unmistakable evidence that the director
of certain fur companies "encouraged the Roman Catholi
priests to go among the Indians and baptize them in orde
that the children of the forest might attain felicity in anothe
world; but they did not plan that the Indian should reac
civilization in this world." [3] On the other hand, there ar
instances where the Indians themselves have been consulte
in advance before missionary work was launched amon
them. An arresting example is that of the Reverend Joh
Sergeant, who in 1734 was appointed by "the Honorabl
Governor of the Colony of Massachusetts Bay, and the Hon

›rable and Reverend Commissioners for Indian Affairs," as nissionary to the Stockbridge Indians. Although Konkapot, he principal chief, was known to approve the Christian re- igion, no mission was started until the Indians themselves ıad been consulted and asked categorically whether they vished to be taught the Christian faith and to have a school or their children. In a speech before a council of the Seneca, Onondaga, and Cayuga tribes, Red Jacket, a sachem of the enecas, "thanks the Society for its work and hopes that it vill continue." [4] There are, of course, other instances where ribes were consulted in advance but refused.

Reviewing the past, any unprejudiced observer cannot help eing profoundly impressed by the value of missionary con- ributions to Indian life. Not only did the missionaries put rimitive languages into writing, thus stimulating literacy nd bilingual expression, but their maps of early explora- ions, manuscripts, and diaries, giving rich detail on the abits, languages, and characteristics of the various tribes, ave aided in preserving historical and geographical material hat might otherwise have been lost.

Ethnologists, historians, linguists, and other scholars have rofited immensely from these pioneer efforts. Included in heir number were the first notable champions of Indian ights, and these, in turn, helped to create "reservoirs of ood will" to offset in marked degree what has often been eferred to as "man's inhumanity to man."

ESTIMONY TO CHRISTIAN CONTRIBUTION

Bearing eloquent witness to these varied contributions are ıcluded such presidents as Theodore Roosevelt, such soldiers s General Howard, such government officials as Commis- oner Francis E. Leupp, such educators as Ray Lyman Wil- ur, such anthropologists as Baron Erland Nordenskiöld, such champions of Indian rights as Elaine Goodale Eastman and Samuel A. Eliot. Said Theodore Roosevelt:

I spent twice the time I intended because I became so intereste as I traveled all over the reservations to see what was being done especially by the missionaries, for it needed no time at all to se that the great factors in the uplifting of the Indian were the men who were teaching the Indian to become a Christian citizen.[5]

Said that redoubtable friend of the Indian, General O. O Howard:

Those who have been most successful in civilizing Indians [th missionaries] brought about a gradual separation from savage way of living and introduced various peaceful industries among them.

Continuing, he cites a specific instance:

A few years ago the quarrels and fights among these Indians wer dreadful, often ending in bloodshed and death, but quarreling ha now altogether ceased, order and cleanliness prevailed, and ther were no more blackened and disfigured faces. Of course, they ha not at that time attained a very high Christian life, but vast an rapid progress had been made.[6]

Perhaps no Commissioner of Indian Affairs showed greater interest in missions to the Indians than did Franci E. Leupp, who writes:

To subdue the Indians, government money was poured out lik water, Indians were slaughtered and white men were slaughtered and nothing was gained except resentful submission to force; bu there were those who believed in "a more excellent way." There i a power greater than that of armies, the power that can chang the hearts and lives of men, even those called savages, and mak them friends; this they knew. They knew that subjugation is a fa cry from civilization and that Christianity alone has the secret o life which carries with it all the motives and conditions of a tru and permanent civilization.[7]

The revered president emeritus of Leland Stanford, whose ontacts with our western Indians have been close and intinate, says:

> There are two agencies through which the Indian has had his nost intimate contact with the white man's civilization—the hristian missionaries and the representatives of the government. f the two, the missionaries, for considerably more than a century, ere in advance of the government agent. They knew the Indian efore the government existed. They were with him when the govrnment was young and before it had given any organized attention o his needs. The only schools he could attend up to half a century go were the mission schools. Missionaries alone for many decades ere his doctors, his agricultural and industrial instructors. They ave worked side by side with the government's representatives ever ince the government began its organized efforts in the fields of ndian education, health, and welfare. They are still at work on nost reservations.[8]

The noted ethnologist, Baron Erland Nordenskiöld, an auhority on the Indians of the two Americas, uses the followng language:

> We know full well that all Indian tribes will sooner or later uccumb to our culture. That is part of the evolutionary process. acing this inevitability, it is, therefore, best that those who first stablish contact with them are missionaries, for they come to give nd not to take.[9]

Mrs. Elaine Goodale Eastman, author, early-day Indian chool supervisor, and present-day protagonist of Indian ights, writes:

> G. Lowes Dickinson has written: "Civilization is a whole. Its art, ts religion, its way of life, all hang together with its economic and echnical development." Christian missionaries have worked on this rinciple, especially among our American Indians. They have been

the first and best civilizers, early realizing that no primitive cultur can long persist side by side with an aggressive machine civilization.[1]

The following tribute from a long-time friend of th Indian who served as a member as well as chairman of th U. S. Board of Indian Commissioners for over twenty year may provide a fitting close to this section:

> In all this transition [from the early colonial days to the present the Christian missionaries have been the pioneer adventurers. The have been, from the earliest Jesuit missions in Canada down to th present day, teaching and preaching and praying and helping. The have tried to champion the rights of the Indian and to protect him not always of course successfully, from wrong. Too much of th record of the white man's relation to the primitive Americans fo the last three centuries has been humiliating, not to say revolting but the resolute persistence of missionary endeavor has been a brigh page in a dark history. It is often, to be sure, a tale of patheti failure. Often the missions have been obliterated as the tide o migration swept westward, or the best efforts of the missionarie have been defeated by the cruelty and rapacity of the conquerin race; but still it is a splendid story that well deserves to be retold.[1]

EVANGELISM AND CHRISTIAN NURTURE

That the missionary of the Cross came into the wildernes with the Bible in one hand and a textbook in the other is well authenticated fact. One of the first concerns of th gospel messengers was the founding of schools.[12] Hand i hand with these educational efforts went the task of trans lation. After acquiring the language of the natives—often long, hard pull—that of putting it into writing followed Textbooks, leading off with a primer, and then portions o the Scriptures, sometimes the entire Bible, were translated Often this involved not only filling old words with new meanings but introducing in some instances virtually a new religious vocabulary. It is a well known fact that the connotations of "sin" and "forgiveness" were absent in many Indian languages. Furthermore, translation meant also a personalizing of religious concepts.[13]

In all this, wise and understanding missionaries sought to build upon the past, for here and there an inkling of a higher power seems to have broken through the dim consciousness of religious belief, perhaps reaching its highest expression in what an Inca thought of the Sun God. "We are told," he said, "that the sun has made all things. But this cannot be; for many things happen when he is absent. He behaves neither like a living thing, for he never tires, nor like a free thing, for he never varies his path. Therefore, the sun must have his master, greater than he; which greater god we ought to worship." [14]

To the people of the wilderness the printed page appeared almost miraculous and savored of the supernatural. And since the Christian religion seemed to be a religion of the book, it came to be called in some languages "the white man's book of heaven," even as his religion was referred to as "the white man's religion." Consider, then, with what amazement the Indian for the first time heard the word of God read in his own tongue. And when one of his own tribesmen was able not only to read but to interpret the printed word, then indeed did a new light break upon his spiritual horizon as he realized that the Bible was intended for the red man as well, a guide along new trails, a lamp unto his feet, a light unto his path. Indicative of this is the testimony attributed to old Monatave, a chief of the Mojaves: "When you read out of that Book, I know it is God's book, for it pulls at my heartstrings." [15]

Among the more notable Bible translations on record are the printing of the Cherokee Scriptures in the Sequoya syllabary in 1831, the Nez Percé Bible in 1871, and the complete Dakota Bible in 1879. The Scriptures, either wholly or in part, have appeared in forty-six languages of the Indian peoples of the United States and Canada. Perhaps the most industrious work in Bible translation during recent years has gone forward in the Southwest, especially in Navajo land where large numbers are still non-English-speaking and isolated.

A most significant contribution to Bible translation in Canada was the perfection of the Cree Syllabic in 1836 by James Evans, a missionary of the British Wesleyans. In the syllabic characters Evans helped to provide a written language quite simple and adequate. Even to this day, a publication known as *Spiritual Light* is issued quarterly in the Cree syllabary and widely used. The Church of England in Canada has also made notable contributions in the translation of the Scriptures into Indian languages, the work of the Reverend F. A. O'Meara, who in 1841 translated much of the Prayer Book and the Bible into Ojibway, being outstanding.

Inasmuch as Indians, in common with most folk, enjoy singing, missionaries have made much of this in encouraging translations of psalms and hymns, not only translated but often composed by the Indians themselves. Consequently, there is extant a considerable hymnology. It is to be noted that this obtains even though there may be no translation of the Scriptures available. Thus we have the Dakota Hymnal, perhaps more pretentious than some of the others, and hymns and songs in the various tribal languages referred to in the foregoing as well as among smaller tribal groupings.

INDIAN EDUCATION IN CANADA

Even to a greater degree than in the United States, Indian education in Canada has been mission-centered, having its beginnings in the efforts of the early missionaries who followed close on the heels of the Hudson's Bay Company, in fact if not actually sponsored by this great fur-trading enterprise of pioneer days. Thus, the origin of the so-called residential schools in western Canada was largely due to the appointment in 1820 of the Reverend John West by the Hudson's Bay Company to act as chaplain to the Red River Settlement (as Winnipeg was then known).

Long before the advent of the residential schools, however, the Society for the Propagation of the Gospel received its first appeal from Canada in the interests of the Indians. This came from Nova Scotia in 1711 and was heeded sixteen years later when a chaplain "was granted ten pounds a year as an allowance for teaching the poor children there." [16] Such ancient and revered societies as the S.P.G. and the S.P.C.K. (Society for Propagating Christian Knowledge) pioneered the way for Christian missionary work among the aboriginal peoples of the Dominion. Another impetus was given to Indian education with the formation of the Church Missionary Society, as already noted. Then, too, with the advent of settlers from New England as well as from the mother country, several denominations, such as the Congregationalists, Methodists, Presbyterians, and Baptists, launched missions in which and through which "teaching wigwams"—as some of the older Indians designated schools—were established where children were taken "to see writing."

From such beginnings, the Indian school system in Canada has developed until today there are 80 residential schools, 275 day schools, about 10 improved day schools, and 10 combined white and Indian schools. These schools are divided among Roman Catholic, Anglican, United Church of Canada, Baptist, Presbyterian (Independent), and one or two other religious bodies. The total capacity of the residential schools in 1939 was 8,518, while that of the day schools totaled 8,427, making an aggregate of 16,945.

There has always been close cooperation of church and government in the Dominion, and Canada has expressed in law her belief in religious education, although the first appropriation by the government for Indian education was not made until 1870. Thus, in the earlier days the missionary sought not only to evangelize the pagan tribes but also to instruct their children without the benefit of government aid. Today, the Department of Indian Affairs at Ottawa (operating under the Minister of Mines and Resources) has a Schools Branch, which looks after the various needs of Indian education. Wherever possible the same course of study is followed as that in use for provincial schools. Public school inspectors also include Indian schools in their supervisory schedules.

The per capita cost of the residential schools (1941) is given at $176. In the United States, the per capita cost for a boarding school of fewer than two hundred pupils is $335. Consequently in practically all the Canadian schools the difference must be made up by grants from such missionary agencies as Sunday schools, Bible classes, and women's auxiliaries. While some degree of success has been recorded in preparing Indian boys and girls for entrance examinations to high school, the progress has been slow and disappointing. The same is true of matriculation for college courses. As a consequence educational leaders have time and again voiced their conviction that provision should be made "for the brighter and more discerning pupils to continue their training and qualify for any profession or commercial position they might desire to follow." [17] As a matter of fact, native leadership in Canada has lagged, partly because Indian pupils quit school at the age of fifteen to return to the reserves with little or no incentive to continue education in higher institutions of learning. What apparently is needed is to get Indian young people "out into the melting pot," away from the static tribalism and the complacency fostered by paternalism.

Furthermore, while all those conversant with the residential schools agree that habits of punctuality and regularity are fostered, that Christian ethics are inculcated, that devoted teaching in the classrooms obtains, that practical instruction in the fundamentals of homemaking and agriculture is stressed, nevertheless the time is at hand in a number of provinces where the shift of emphasis should be made to the day schools, especially in districts where homes are stable and reasonably compact. In fact, the day school may very well serve as a stabilizing influence in Indian community life. Too often the residential schools, as is true also in the United States, inadvertently deprive the parents of the oversight and maintenance that rightfully belong to them.

The missionary work centering around schools, residential as well as day, has accomplished much in a comparatively short space of time, considering the pioneer aspects of the task. The span from the old paganism to the present development covers only a few decades. Illiteracy, industrial backwardness, frontier lawlessness and vice, the isolation and segregation of reserve life, certain tribal customs and practices—all have stood menacingly in the pathway of the red man's advance. In some respects the Indian has traveled little beyond the first milestone, but he is pressing on.

With this background it is but natural that the church

societies strongly recommend a long-range policy in the matter of Indian education—one that will not be subject to change with every shift of government.

To them, the Indian problem is only a part of that much greater problem that embraces the education of indigenous peoples throughout the whole world. Instead of calling them "Indian problems," these should be recognized as purely human problems, and all efforts exerted to solve them in much the same way adopted with other groups and communities now domiciled within the Canadian shores. The report on Indian Education previously cited goes on to say:

> If it be taken for granted—and the church societies can see no alternative in the matter—that the Indian peoples of this country are destined to share the responsibilities as well as the privileges of full and unrestricted citizenship, then the whole future policy of the educational system on their behalf must be shaped and controlled with this objective clearly in view. The achievement of ultimate success will require great care in the drafting of the details of the policy itself, and a spirit of patience, good will, and mutual understanding on the part of those engaged to carry it into effect. Progress at the start may be slow, but as soon as the blighting suspicions of the present have given way to a wholesome confidence, it will increase in momentum until the periods of transition and adjustment have been successfully passed, and assimilation has been attained.

MEDICAL MISSIONS

The church has also pioneered in medical missionary work. That the introduction of modern medicine, sanitation, and healing was no easy task has already been pointed out.[18] The power and influence of the medicine men had to be reckoned with, for they were believed to have secret knowledge of things occult and through magic to control these powers and use them in ceremonial healing. Even today these *shamans* exercise strong influence among certain tribes, markedly so among the Navajos.

The contribution of medical missions, though never launched on an extensive scale, has been a notable one. During early days, the missionary often undertook the threefold task of evangelist, teacher, and doctor. Where hospitals could not be erected, clinics were maintained and first aid freely administered. At present the Sage Memorial Hospital at Ganado, Arizona, is the outstanding medical mission in Indian country. Accredited by the American College of Surgeons, this institution of one hundred and fifty beds, well staffed with doctors and nurses, maintains the only training school in the United States for Indian nurses. The nurses' school is accredited by the state and the American Medical Association, and is listed with the National League of Nursing Education. In 1942 there were enrolled forty students, representing twenty-eight tribes. The superintendent of the Ganado Mission, Dr. Clarence G. Salsbury, known far and wide as "the big white medicine man," speaking on behalf of his work and that of his colleagues, says, in part:

> There are no marble halls or terraced floors in Sage Memorial Hospital at Ganado, but it is a well planned, businesslike hospital and its beds are usually full. . . . All the nurses are high school graduates; most of them are mission school graduates. . . . They are not preparing to be nurses just because they want to do something different or to earn a livelihood, but because they have seen a vision of how they may serve Christ that way. . . . Extension service, in the shape of a medical field program, is carried on by the hospital within a radius of thirty miles.

Continuing, Dr. Salsbury strikes the keynote when he says:

> The Indian is not a creature apart from the rest of humanity, but is one of God's children, with human problems and passions, with

a body and mind and soul all hungering and thirsting for the best life of which he is capable. The door of the *hogan*, facing the rising sun, is symbolical of the door of hope, of faith, of opportunity for the Navajo nation—the greatest of all Indian tribes in America.[19]

NATIVE LEADERSHIP

While the early missionaries were concerned about the education of the children, the healing of the sick, and the comforting of the afflicted, their primary objective was the proclamation of the gospel. In order to do this most effectively, however, they fully realized the paramount importance of discovering, training, and using native leadership. In this connection, more than one experienced missionary has voiced the following sentiment: "The constant testimony of the Indian preacher to Christian teaching and Christian things, just because it is from an Indian, is worth more than any amount of preaching from a white man." Historically, the most successful missions are those in which Indians have actively participated in the evangelization of their own people.

Then, too, while an appreciable number of white missionaries have mastered and effectively used the native languages, it was felt that where the tribe was small in numbers and situated near white settlements, Indian interpreters could be trained sufficiently to take care of bilingual expression, thus obviating the necessity of the missionary's learning and using the vernacular. This arrangement, while perhaps justified as a temporary expedient, was by no means ideal (as those who have had occasion to use interpreters very well know), for it was extremely difficult to convey the "heart" of the message, not to speak of imbuing the listeners with the proper spirit, through the medium of interpretation.

Whether a missionary was proficient or not in the tribal

language, he realized that "every race in the end must be elevated by its own educated leadership," a leadership inspired and permeated by the Christian motive. Reference has already been made to the contribution of mission schools in developing Christian leaders. However, there are outstanding examples of prominent leaders in the old Indian life who on accepting the teachings of the gospel, though unable to read or write in any language, have become staunch Christian leaders among their respective tribes. Time and again these devoted servants of Christ have demonstrated that force of character, determination, and, above all, consecration can overcome educational lack.

But from the very beginning of the missionary enterprise the need for special schools to train native leaders, offering courses in religious subjects, was keenly felt. One of the most distinctive and successful of these "schools of the prophets" was that launched at the McBeth Mission at Lapwai, Idaho, among the Nez Percés. As early as 1873 Miss Sue L. McBeth began training a native ministry. In 1879, her sister Kate joined her and the work grew apace; later in 1895 Miss Mary M. Crawford, a niece of the McBeth sisters, came as assistant and remained forty-five years. During all that time ministers, elders, Sunday school superintendents, and other leaders have received their training under the auspices of that mission, which had no pretentious buildings of which to boast, no learned theological professors to show off, no academic degrees to offer. Not only were the Nez Percés admitted to the four-year course but representatives from such neighboring tribes as the Makah, Spokane, Umatilla, and Walla Walla. Miss Crawford, commenting on this work, says:

> The Nez Percé ministers take their places in the presbytery beside the white ministers, are made responsible for the work of their own

> churches and report direct to the presbytery, and have taken equally as good care of their churches for the last forty and more years; and we are hoping that those from other tribes will have the same status.
>
> Many tribes are calling for the Nez Percé ministers, not only our own denomination [Presbyterian], but Mennonites, Methodists, Baptists, and United Presbyterians, and our men draw no denominational lines and are welcomed everywhere. Is it any wonder that we are all believers in a Christian *native leadership?* [20]

In course of time the McBeth school was closed as it was felt that the school had served its purpose. There comes a time in every mission when the young people should be encouraged to leave the reservations to continue their education elsewhere inasmuch as "new occasions teach new duties," a new type of preparation, and in a new setting.

Another fruitful endeavor in the field of training a native leadership was that advocated in the early nineties by the veteran missionary to the Pimas, Charles H. Cook. It was not until 1910 that his dream was realized, a training center being opened the following year at Tucson, Arizona, under the name of the Cook Bible School; it was later moved to its present site at Phoenix. Among the various tribes represented in the student body from time to time have been Pima, Papago, Mojave, Maricopa, Yavapai, Sac and Fox, Nez Percé, Choctaw, Cherokee, Chemehuevi, Comanche, Yuma, Hopi, Apache, Navajo, Sioux, and Winnebago.

Launched under Presbyterian auspices, this school has in recent years become interdenominational and is maintained under the auspices of the Home Missions Council. A curriculum designed to be at once practical and adequate is being worked out. This training institute now aims to provide a school center with good living and teaching facilities that will not only give classroom instruction but also provide pportunities for supervised service among Indians living in he vicinity and, whenever desirable, the privilege of taking cademic work of college level in near-by institutions. The econd aspect of the training program contemplates a sort of "school on wheels," to carry an extension program to groups of Indian workers who would otherwise be beyond the each of the training center. Needless to say, this new inter-denominational enterprise, now known as the Charles H. Cook Christian Training School, will be followed with interest by all advocates of native leadership training throughout he entire Indian country.

Aside from specific schools, leadership training by correspondence courses has been instituted. This method has been specially noteworthy in the Sioux country, the Episcopalians developing the Niobrara course and the Congregationalists and Presbyterians, the Santee Bible courses. In the Chippewa country some success has been reported in following the "interneship method," whereby a few promising candidates spend the winter months studying with the missionary pastor. These methods have invariably been used with native-speaking personnel. In recent years a marked change is evident, from training native-speaking older people in their own language to sponsoring younger men through college and seminary. In the Sioux country, where native-speaking churches have developed in past decades, the emphasis is increasingly on facility in the use of English as well as Dakota. The feeling is general that in another generation English can be used almost exclusively in all church services, even as it is already the medium of expression in church and secular schools.

In eastern Oklahoma, the habitat of the Five Civilized Tribes, one naturally expects to find native workers dedicated to the cause of evangelization. Such institutions as Bacone, Dwight, Old Goodland, Oklahoma Presbyterian College, Oklahoma Baptist University, and the American Indian Institute (now closed) have all had a part in preparing and sending forth many of the present generation of Christian leaders, lay as well as clerical.

NATIONAL FELLOWSHIP OF INDIAN WORKERS

To give further impetus to in-service training of missionaries as well as to stimulate native leadership there was organized at the University of Wisconsin in connection with the Rural Leadership Summer School, 1935, the National Fellowship of Indian Workers. Implicit in its purpose and program is the aim "to establish and to foster a unity of spirit and service among Indian missionaries, mission board members, government employees, and other friends of the Indian to affirm their group consciousness, to share their experiences and to establish orderly means to discuss any matters affecting the welfare of Indians and Indian missions." Through conferences and its quarterly bulletin this organization has already made noteworthy contributions toward interracial good will as well as promoting factual studies on peyote and wardship It is significant that the national president is an Indian while several regional officers of the six areas, especially in Oklahoma, are Indians, well trained and qualified for their tasks Following his attendance at the 1942 regional conferences President Robert P. Chaat of the Comanche tribe, an ordained minister, wrote an appraisal of the work made possible by this agency:

> The National Fellowship of Indian Workers is an organization that very definitely meets a need. It has drawn us of the Indian work together as nothing else has done. It has encouraged and helped the Indians, who have so often seen division, instead o

ellowship and cooperation, in the mission field. We have learned o know one another; we can pray more intelligently for the whole ndian work and share together our problems as well as rejoice in ur accomplishments. Then, too, it has enabled board members and xecutives to attend the various conferences and to meet the workrs on the field; also to know other workers. The fine contributions rom the Home Missions Council and various church and mission oards have helped the workers.[21]

NATIVE PARTICIPATION STILL LAGGING

While much of the work of Indian evangelization today is arried on by native leaders, it does not necessarily mean that he number of native pastors and evangelists exceeds that of white missionary workers; however, when there are included hose who act as interpreters, catechists, lay helpers, young nd old, in Sunday schools, women's societies, and young people's organizations, the total figure is an impressive one. Nor is this work limited to what goes on within the four walls of a church building. Missionaries have from the very beginning made use of the Indian's social tendencies by reconstituting the old-time gatherings into camp meetings, convocations, and conferences, often in brush arbors or tents or under the open sky. Here the women frequently outdo he men in their attendance, contributions, and concrete expressions of service. It hardly needs to be added that this situation is not peculiar to American Indian Christianity. The various women's organizations, under whatever name or banner, in friendly rivalry at times, vie with one another in bringing in reports that will show larger gifts of money for the promotion of the gospel than the year before, often in he face of discouraging drought conditions and financial lepression.

It must be kept in mind that Indian participation, though

a cause for rejoicing, is still somewhat sporadic and far from being an accomplished fact. In recent years considerable pres sure has been brought to bear on Indian youth to enter othe than full-time Christian callings. The more attractive wag scale as well as the apparent financial security offered by cer tain secular vocations naturally furnish a strong appeal. Need less to say, this is not peculiar to Indian people, young or old Furthermore, an equalization of salaries for Indian pastors in order to insure a living wage, is a crying need on the par of Christian agencies.

Progress will continue to be slow unless missionary leader with greater earnestness recruit, train, and release an increas ingly larger number of native workers for the evangelization of their own people.

AN INDIAN MISSION BECOMES A CHURCH

In the program of Indian evangelization there are certain stages of development that may be recognized. First, there is the Indian mission, often encountering as it gets under way opposition from the adherents of the old tribal religion or of such pseudo-cults as Peyotism and Shakerism. There is much ground work to be done, such as house-to-house, *hogan*-to-*hogan*, camp-to-camp visitation over a period of years. The organization of a local church must await developments.

Then follows the next stage, with a group of believers gathered for worship, using the native language, perhaps having "interpreted" services, with here and there a native leader taking part, generally under the tutelage of the white missionary. From such a group may spring a definite Christian fellowship, eventuating in church organization. Native leaders will in due time be trained to carry on. There evolves gradually the type of church developed among such tribes as the Chippewa, Sioux, Nez Percé, Cherokee, Choctaw,

Creek, Seminole, Comanche, Kiowa; and more recently in the Southwest among the Pima, Mojave, and, to a limited extent, among the Hopi and Navajo. For example, the Methodists have what is known as "The Indian Mission of Oklahoma." There are an annual conference, 3 districts, 33 Indian pastors, 3 district superintendents, 1 general superintendent, ,855 members. In the area served by these churches the Indians comprise almost the total population and these Indian pastors have been doing some very effective work under the leadership of district superintendents, several of whom are Indians.

With the spread of public schools and the exclusive use of the English language in practically all government and mission schools, the children acquire a new tongue and become used to hearing sermons in that language as well as participating in religious activities during school days. The inevitable next step is the church in which services are conducted in English, often under trained Indian leadership, the non-English-speaking constituency either provided with separate or interpreted services. Here the transition should not be too abrupt for the sake of the older people who have borne the burden and heat of other days. For it must be remembered that in the old order great respect was paid to age, and youth was rarely accorded a place in the councils of the elders.

Where reservations have been "opened up" for many years —and an overwhelming majority are in that class—the Indians have rubbed elbows with their white neighbors in many phases of community life, public schools, village stores, voting booths, recreation centers, civic and social gatherings. The process of assimilation has been going forward so that a common bond of community interest has developed. As a result there should come into being a church in which Indian and white people worship together, mingling freely in Chris-

tian fellowship as children of a common Father. This churc
may or may not be under Indian leadership, as far as th
pastorate is concerned. It may or may not be self-sustainin
and free from home mission subsidy, but the goal will defi
nitely be set in that direction. Naturally a church organiza
tion of this sort makes possible a more fruitful associatio
with other churches in the immediate vicinity as well as out
side, thus promoting a better cooperative spirit than the iso
lated, segregated church. Of even more importance, a churc
of this kind paves the way for a Christian assimilation int
American life.

Having traced the foregoing steps, it would seem that
separate or indigenous church for most Indian people is no
called for at this time. However, there are areas, remote an
isolated, where such churches may function fruitfully fo
years to come. Perhaps the outstanding example of this situa
tion is to be found among the Navajos. Twenty-five year
ago, following a field survey of that area, the writer urge
that "at every mission station a small group of promisin
native leaders should be trained for missionary service in th
future." Wherever these conditions have been met certai
results have followed. But alas, after fifty years of missionar
effort among these people one can count on the fingers of on
hand the number of full-time native Christian leaders.

The Christian mission among the Navajos still waits for a
Indian Moses who can lead these gifted people from the wild
erness of sterile *shamanism*, sometimes referred to as the medi
cine man cult of "sings," into the promised land of Christia
discipleship. As the desert cries out for water and bring
forth abundantly when water is given, so are the hearts o
this people thirsting for God, ready to respond with th
fruits of life when they have the water of life for refresh
ment. However, some progress, not only in the training o

native leaders, but in developing local autonomous churches, has been made in recent years.

While independent agencies have in certain respects taken the initiative, the denominational agencies that have sustained a long-time relationship, such as the Presbyterian, Methodist, Episcopal, and Christian Reformed, also have initiated programs which, although slow in maturing, should prove helpful. It is to be emphasized that all have made a distinctive contribution over a period of years, one agency stressing Christian education, another medical missions, still another the evangelistic, or "camp" work.

Reference has already been made to the medical service of the Presbyterians in Navajo land. The Episcopalians, while not neglecting that phase of missions, have at times stressed the work among orphans. The Methodist Mission School at Farmington, New Mexico, is a monument to educational missions. Launched in the nineties in a one-room adobe building with a dozen pupils, it has developed into a fully accredited grade and high school, with splendid equipment and personnel. A declared aim is "to train students for Christian service, especially emphasizing the need among their own people."

While all have done something in the field of church organization, the Christian Reformed mission has perhaps gone further recently in drawing up a blueprint of procedure for the reorganization of its churches with the aim of making them more truly indigenous. In summing up the 1942 report of the Synodical Committee on Native Churches on the Indian Field, the following language is used:

> It is through these sanctified native powers that Christ would evangelize the nation itself. A tribe can best be leavened from within. We believe that the sanctified native characteristics of the

Navajo and Zuñi Christians may and should contribute to the beauty of the Indian church, not for reasons of display but rather for the enrichment of their Christian fellowship in a native setting.

This effort to build up local, self-governing churches in Navajo land will be followed with growing interest, for it should, among other things, lead to a revival of the spiritual capacities of a people long dominated by a religion of fear.

RELIGIOUS WORK IN GOVERNMENT SCHOOLS

The first great crisis in an Indian child's life comes when he leaves the reservation home to enter school. Here he finds himself in an alien atmosphere. As a rule, he does not yet appreciate the necessity of an education. The details of school life seem many and complex. It is then he most needs a wise and patient guide, to interpret for him the significance of these new and strange relationships. Fortunately for the child, the government Indian Service personnel has in the face of captious and often unjust criticism helped surprisingly well to tide him over this difficult period. All honor to hundreds of devoted, consecrated teachers, matrons, advisors, and others, whether in high positions or low, who, actuated by Christian motives, have carried on their thankless tasks despite long hours, low salaries, and isolated surroundings.

It goes without saying that these schools have always offered a most challenging field to Christian service. In fact, until very recent years, the government delegated the religious education of the Indian boys and girls in these schools to the churches, Protestant as well as Catholic. Thus, while the particular teachings of the several denominations were given in groups meeting under their respective auspices and while proselyting was strictly forbidden, a fine spirit of cooperation and good will for the most part characterized the relationships existing between government and church agencies. More than one Indian Commissioner has paid tribute to the value of Christian teaching. As recently as 1931, the then Commissioner, the Honorable Charles J. Rhoads, in communicating with the superintendents and all employees of the Indian Service, emphasized this relationship in no uncertain language:

> The aim of both Indian Service employees and church workers is to fit the Indians to be self-sustaining, self-respecting American citizens. The Christian missionary was active in this field of service long before the government, and the missionary has an essential function in the cultural development of the Indian. No effort should be spared to encourage effective cooperation and prevent misunderstanding and friction. Religious education and character training are necessary factors in the development of the Indians.[22]

However, with the change in administration in 1933 came a reversal in policy, not only with respect to government aims for the Indian Service, as noted elsewhere, but also changes in rules and regulations affecting religious instruction. These involved definite restrictions, not only as to time and place but including the method, previously discarded, of securing written signatures from the parents (or guardians) in the presence of government officials before Indian children could be released for such instruction.[23] This was a striking contrast to the usual encouragement reiterated in previous regulations, namely, "Pupils are expected to attend the respective churches to which they belong or for which their parents or guardians express a preference." [24]

The abrupt changes in policy threw Indian parents into confusion, filled the minds of the field personnel with apprehension and uncertainty, and did much to undermine the morale of the Indian Service.

Despite regulations and restrictions, religious work has been going forward, if not with the enthusiasm of former years, nevertheless with a fair degree of regularity in some places, intermittently in others. In certain areas where government day schools are in operation, the field missionary or his assistants promote religious instruction by weekly visits. The plan is somewhat similar to weekday religious education carried on in other communities. The boarding schools on the reservations, however, must be served by workers coming in from the outside, who must be prepared to sandwich in their classes at such leisure time as the pupils may have.

With respect to the non-reservation schools, such as Haskell, Chilocco, Flandreau, Phoenix, Sherman, Carson, and Chemawa, the situation is somewhat different. Here students often enroll from several states and represent many tribes and reservations. Naturally they come from areas where various denominations have been at work, and as a consequence their church affiliations are varied. Here a united interdenominational approach has a compelling appeal, for it would be impossible for each church to have its own workers.

Before the churches were adequately organized to launch a program of religious education under trained leadership, the national organization of the Young Men's Christian Association and the Young Women's Christian Association rendered valuable service in this field. In some places, notably Riverside, California, the local churches organized themselves into a federation to cooperate in the work of these schools. Since 1919, with the appointment of the first religious work director at Haskell, the churches have pooled their interests through the Indian Committee of the Home Missions Council of North America. They thus presented, perhaps for the first time in Indian as well as home missionary history, a united front. In eight of the larger schools these trained workers are the churches' representatives, and, with local cooperation, seek to adapt their programs to meet the needs of each particular school. When schools are conveniently situated, opportunity is provided for each student enrolled to know the work of his own denomination and to become affiliated with it. At the smaller schools where one denomination may be strong numerically, sometimes making possible a grouping of all the Protestant students in one unit, the work may be assigned to the religious oversight of that particular church; in still others, neighboring pastors or missionaries assist as they can.

In government schools, as elsewhere, less time is available for the actual study of religion than for any other subject. And yet, the director may find it possible to radiate a Christian spirit that will permeate every activity with religion. With a large number of students in their middle teens, away from home for the first time, he finds himself in the position of parent and pastor and carries on his service regardless of denominational lines. He is called upon to stimulate, correlate, and promote the religious work of the various agencies on or near the campus. His program, while flexible, must be directed toward some long-range objectives as well as toward immediately observable results. In his teaching work, he seeks to give a thorough grounding in the Bible so that at least some of his students will be encouraged to prepare to serve as teachers in their home communities. A wise and understanding leader gave expression to this as follows: "As I think of the needs of Indian boys and girls, I am more concerned each day that we should bring to them larger knowledge of the Bible; that we should store their memories with more that will help them through the long silences and the days that are hard. They need to know the stories of the early Christians who dared be true to Jesus in the midst of pagan surroundings."

In all this the religious worker endeavors to make religion a functional part of school life so that students will naturally take positions of responsibility in the program and so fit themselves for religious leadership.

That Indian students are willing and eager to assume responsibility and fit into a program that challenges the best in them is the testimony of those whose long experience qualifies them to speak. They welcome an opportunity to lead meetings, speak in public, pray, and sing. They enjoy going out to surrounding communities to put on programs in churches, clubs, and schools. Some are beginning to feel at home and to share thinking and responsibilities with the leaders and members of youth organizations. Our American system of conferences makes a great appeal to them. Not only have Indian students for many years been regular attendants at summer camps and conferences, youth institutes and rallies, at home and occasionally abroad, but they have actively participated as featured speakers, advisers, and leaders.

Religious work in government schools has resulted not only in changed lives but in a changed outlook toward Christian leadership. Said a Cherokee: "The old people look up to us, the educated ones. They believe we can lead. We fail often because we do not prepare right. Christian students can lead."

Yes, Indian students can lead; they have already demonstrated that. Among the men and women who have gone out from the schools are community builders, educators, doctors, nurses, lawyers, farmers, preachers, teachers, mechanics, clerks, interpreters, homemakers; some are still in active service; others have already gone to their reward. Among the latter may be mentioned the late Isaac Greyearth, member of the first gospel team at Haskell and serving as the first Religious Work Director at Flandreau, who used to say, "No matter what skill of hand or training of mind I may have, unless I have Jesus Christ in my heart, I cannot stand." He stood the test as a Christian leader among his people, and today his name is still held in reverence by all those who came under his influence.

When gold nuggets are found men say, "There is more gold here to be mined," and so they keep digging. So also when nuggets of character are found. Indian boys and girls are like nuggets and gems. As we mine here we see the hand of God at work on raw material. He would enlist us, our resources in prayer and money, in this character-finding, character-developing enterprise. For an Indian leader of his race has wisely said: "Health, education, and character are outstanding needs of the Indian today, but the greatest of these is character."

REFERENCES

1. Incorporated November 19, 1787, by the Commonwealth of Massachusetts and known as "the oldest incorporated missionary society in America."
2. *Matthew* 28:18, from *The Bible: A New Translation,* by James Moffatt. Harper & Brothers, publishers.
3. *The Oregon Missions,* by Bishop James Whitford Bashford, p. 53. New York, Abingdon Press, 1918.
4. *Annual Report of the New York Missionary Society,* 1804, p. 89.
5. Theodore Roosevelt in an address to the Ecumenical Conference on Foreign Missions, New York, 1900.
6. *My Life and Experiences among the Hostile Indians,* by O. O. Howard, pp. 11, 319. Hartford, Connecticut, A. D. Worthington & Co., 1907.
7. *In Red Man's Land,* by Francis E. Leupp, p. 148. New York, Fleming H. Revell Co., 1914.
8. "Continuing Cooperation in a New Program," by Ray Lyman Wilbur, in *The American Missionary,* September 4, 1930. Boston, Massachusetts.
9. *Indianer och Vita,* av Erland Nordenskiöld, p. 150. Stockholm, Bonniers Forlag, 1911.

10. "Why Discriminate against Indians?" by Elaine Goodale Eastman, in *The Watchman Examiner,* September 26, 1935.
11. "Society for Propagating the Gospel among the Indians and Others in North America, An Historical Sketch," by Samuel A. Eliot, in *Proceedings of Massachusetts Historical Society,* 1937, Vol. 66, p. 111. Boston.
12. See Chapter V.
13. In this connection it is significant to note that there were no "swear words" in the Indian tongues.
14. Quoted in *The Meaning of God in Human Experience,* by W. E. Hocking, p. 325. New Haven, Yale University Press, 1923.
15. Quoted in "The Bible in the Life of the Indians of the United States," by Thomas C. Moffett, p. 21. New York, American Bible Society, 1916.
16. *Inasmuch,* by S. Gould, p. 131. Toronto, The Missionary Society of the Church of England, 1917.
17. "Indian Education: Suggestions for Improving the Prevailing System," presented to the Minister of Mines and Resources, November 21, 1939.
18. See Chap. IV.
19. "Christ Comes to the Navajo," by Clarence G. Salsbury, in *The Missionary Review of the World,* February, 1937, pp. 79, 80.
20. Quoted in "Christian Missions among the American Indians," Bulletin No. 280, p. 22. U. S. Board of Indian Commissioners, Washington.
21. *News-Letter,* October, 1942, No. 19, published at Room 69, 297 Fourth Ave., New York.
22. Indian Office Letter of May 21, 1931.
23. Commissioner's Circular of January 15, 1934.
24. Rules of the Indian School Service, No. 129, p. 16.

Chapter VII

THE INDIAN'S PART IN TOMORROW'S WORLD

"IN THE WORLD OF TOMORROW, THE INDIAN WILL HOLD the place of his own choosing." These words of a Choctaw Indian educator, Mr. J. H. Belvin, Superintendent f Schools in Bryan County, Oklahoma, were uttered at the losing session of the Oklahoma Regional Conference of the Jational Fellowship of Indian Workers held at Bacone Colege, June, 1943. They are pregnant with meaning and prohetic of the part Indian Americans will play in tomorrow's vorld.

Mr. Belvin echoes the sentiments of all those who realize hat the Indian is standing on the threshold of a new era from vhich there is no turning back. Ahead of him he understands hat there is to be all that is epitomized in the phrase "full articipation in American life." He did not refuse to fight ecause he was, and still is, a ward. In New Mexico, for xample, the Indians were called to the colors as were other itizens. They were in the front-line trenches at Bataan and n the fox-holes of the Solomon Islands, yet in that very state hey are today denied the right of suffrage, a distinctive mark f citizenship, because they are in a wardship status under he Federal government. Since formal citizenship came to the ndians as a result of their participation in World War I, ave they not a right to anticipate that release from Federal

wardship should be forthcoming as a definite by-product o
World War II? They have often been referred to as "Uncl
Sam's step-children"; must they remain step-children forever

In a similar vein, Mr. Lee F. Harkins, a Choctaw-Chicka
saw, writing in the Rotary magazine, declares that the India
must face reality:

> To keep the Indian Indian, you would have to turn the cloc
> back to restore conditions as they were. Adaptability has eve
> marked Indian history—and ever will. To pine for the old triba
> days is to fly from reality, as the psychologists say. It is a mark o
> weakness, not strength; of cowardice, not courage. The India
> always had some defense against his enemies, but there was no on
> to protect him from his oversentimental friends. I, too, glory i
> the legends, traditions, lore, and art of my people—but my Germa
> and French and Scandinavian neighbors can say the same of their
>
> Let us escape from the reservations: not all at once, of cours
> Despite all its shortcomings, the government's policy has bee
> gradual assimilation of Indians into the civilization that surround
> them. But at the moment, that trend is reversed—and it is agains
> nature and the Indian's welfare. Let us instead be assimilated, le
> us be one of you.[1]

FULL PARTICIPATION IN AMERICAN LIFE

The Indian people today realize that the past order i
beyond recall. The buffalo has long since vanished from th
plains; the great north woods no longer support wild gam
and fur-bearing animals, nor can that area be reforested a
in the days of the French-Canadian fur traders; the lakes an
streams no longer teem with fish, and in some states th
Indians are not allowed to hunt and fish except under th
same limitations imposed on other citizens. It goes withou
saying that the Indian can no longer live in the white man'
world by his old pursuits of hunting and fishing. Even th
native arts, such as bead-work, basketry, pottery, rug weav-

ng, and leather-work, are rapidly being superseded by the ess intricate and arduous, less confining and time-consuming, ndustries of a mechanistic age. Whether his lot is cast on the arm or in the factory, whether he is to follow the plow and njoy the fruits of the soil or weld tanks and assemble air-lanes in urban surroundings, he is increasingly being made ware of the democratic ideal of full participation in Ameri-an life.

A Pima, Harvey Allison, a student at the Phoenix Indian chool, appearing before a conference of CCC Educational Advisors, made a moving plea for this participation on the asis of being "true Americans":

In your schools we have learned the Christian religion. We believe hat we should do unto others as we would have them do unto us. 'ou have taught us to be ambitious, to want to go ahead. All that e ask now is a chance. All too often we find as we go about that eople are prejudiced; that they look down on us as a race. They eel above us. They want nothing to do with us.

My appeal to you tonight is that you give us credit for what we re as individuals, that you forget color, race, and tribe, and treat s as your equals if we behave as your equals.

You have taught us to adopt your customs and modes of living. Ve have learned your trades, we have adopted your mode of dress, ve have been converted to your religion, we speak your language; ve want your friendly cooperation and an opportunity to put into ractice the things that you have taught us. Some of us are inter-sted in farming, others in the building trades, and still others in he mechanical trades.

If you give us this opportunity and we fail, then it is all our ault. You will not be in any way to blame. You will have done our part. But we will not all fail and some day you will be proud f us and glad to know that you had a part in helping us to suc-eed. We are the only true Americans. We want to be American itizens with you.[2]

"IS THE WAY BACK EVER THE WAY OUT?"

At the height of the agitation incident to the propose Wheeler-Howard Bill in 1934, which, among other thing advocated a return to the old tribal life, Ernest Hunt, whos father, the late George Hunt, was well and favorably know as a deacon in the Kiowa Baptist Church in western Okla homa, thus expressed his conviction:

> There are two ways out of this matter, the way back and th way straight ahead. But is the way back ever the way out? The wa back is a way beset with failures, wickedness, and graft. We hav made some advances, but we need encouragement that we may g still farther. If ever the Indian needed the guidance of the Grea Government of Heaven it is now. We need in the very heart of ou councils a friend to the Indians that will advise us right.[3]

Tribalism, insofar as it has militated against united action cooperation, and effective organization, has been weighed i the balances and found wanting. Today it often masquerade under the high-sounding rubric of "the cult of the primi tive." But the old Indian culture, whatever may have bee the merits of "deep beauty, spiritual guidance, consolation and disciplinary power" attributed to it in the past, no longe yields to youth—and here maturity may also be included— the individual and group satisfactions necessary to its perpet uation. Education, conceived in its broadest sense, has per haps been the most important factor in bringing abou changed attitudes. Today are we not seeing the successfu results of that education in the new spirit of the India people that sends them away from home into work, har work and new, by the side of their fellow-citizens?

Other factors promoting the disintegration of the old cere monial life, especially in the Southwest, are such economi changes as the introduction and adoption of the wage system nd the inability of the old culture to develop and use eco-omic resources to support an increasing population on an cceptable level. Perhaps the inconsistency that would lead ne to dance in propitiation of the rain gods and at the same ime rely on the advice of the Department of Agriculture s a bit of mental coordination that present-day Indian youth ttains with difficulty.

Even where tribal life lingers, white civilization is pressing lose. The growth of new towns adjoining reservations, with he ever present cinema and other attractions, the commer-ializing of Indian ceremonies, the rodeos and the fairs, the utomobiles and the radios, the improved highways and the onvenient "five and ten" emporiums, the beauty parlors and he style shops—all have a share in the process of accultura-ion. In short, the radius of the Indian's circle is greater, his orizon wider. His wish to live in isolation from the white nan is no longer a question. He cannot isolate himself if he vould. The Indian is destined to become a part of the life round him.

This is true for Indians on both sides of the international oundary line. The Canadian Indian, in the past more segre-ated and isolated than his red brother in the States, "cannot orever, nor even for many years longer, live a segregated fe, and must eventually either be merged into the white fe of this country, or cease to exist." [4]

LD INDIANS SPEAK THEIR MINDS

Goodbird, of the Fort Berthold Reservation, North Dakota, epresenting an older generation of Hidatsas, sensed the inevi-ability of this change years ago, phrasing it in simple but ointed fashion:

> We know that our Indian ways will soon perish, but we feel no nger. The government has given us a good reservation, and we

think the new way better for our children. I think God made a peoples to help one another. We Indians have helped you whit people. All over this country are cornfields; we Indians gave yo the seeds for your corn (a quickly maturing variety), and we gav you squashes and beans. On the lakes in your parks are canoe Indians taught you to make those canoes.[5]

A few years ago a Chiricahua Apache, also of an olde generation, testifying at a tribal meeting held at Anadark Oklahoma, when certain features of Indian reorganizatio legislation were being considered, said:

I don't know why the government wants to bring us up as whit people and then when we come up as white people they don't like i Somebody say they want to put us way back. I don't want to g back, I got tired of that. I don't want to wear a seventy-five cen suit again. I got white neighbors and I love them. The Bible says t love your neighbors. I don't want to change. When they take m to Alabama [as prisoner of war] General Howard says, "Look u not down; look forward, not backward." I still remember that an I want to go forward.[6]

CAN TRIBALISM BE REVIVED?

As for the revival of tribalism, whether according to Na culture patterns or under the guise of so-called self-govern ment, long-time friends of the Indian as well as the Indian most immediately concerned have time and again place themselves on record. Dr. Fayette A. McKenzie, a membe of the Meriam Commission appointed by a former Secretar of the Interior to survey Indian affairs, says, "Any attemp to turn back the wheels of time and restore tribal govern ment, political, judicial, economic, is doomed to large an destructive failure."[7]

Dr. Arthur C. Parker, co-founder and secretary of th Society of American Indians, himself of Seneca descent, serv ıg now with distinction as director of the Rochester Museum f Arts and Sciences, writes:

While the continuation of tribal government, with all its con- ›tations, may seem, from the sentimental standpoint, just and ›eral, it brings with it also a certain segregation from the normal ream of civic life. . . . This might possibly be justified if their he Indians'] ultimate objective, projected a century hence, was continued separateness in outlook and manner of living. However, ıce all the Indians of the United States must secure a livelihood a manner similar to that of the rest of the population, and since ıeir economic contacts will all be with citizens of the various ates, it would seem that the better part of wisdom is to have ıese Indians prepare in a most effective way for economic com- tence. There is always prejudice against those with special privi- ges and exemptions and against those who are fostered by ıternalism.[8]

Speaking for the Indian south of the Rio Grande, the late r. Moisés Sáenz, distinguished educator, addressing a group Indian school teachers, said, in part:

In Mexico there is no movement to keep him Indian, rather a ing to the Indian to bring him into the national family. As to ıe United States, what do you want the Indian to become? As to hat he might have been, that is past, and can never be recovered. . . Unless you isolate the Indian, I don't see how you can keep m from being influenced. I don't think he will be benefited by ing made a human zoo. The alternative is to loosen him into the ream of national life. This is happening in Mexico.

If you believe them [the Indians] equals, then you treat them responsible, reasoning fellow-humans, able to stand on their own et, and capable of doing for themselves. Instead of indulgence, you t them assume responsibility and challenge their highest abilities. he Indian has been made too much of a dependent. The sooner you t him out of this dependence and on his own, the better.[9]

A native South African, Selby N'gcabo, while a graduat
student at Yale University, made a tour of Indian reservatior
in the Southwest and later addressed an Indian school a
follows:

I am very much impressed with your people over here in th
United States. All the silly notions that I had about seeing Indiar
with feathers disappeared as soon as I saw the first reservation. . .
I am from the big continent of Africa. We are so far away fron
opportunity for an improvement that we remain behind the mar
of other nations—like you people here before the white man cam
in contact with your grandfathers; but now recently all this ha
been changed, or is changing. European merchants, traders, soldier
hunters, and governments set up by Europeans have come alon
and they have a different way of life. *This different way of lif
creates a pressure but this pressure uplifts.* That is why you see m
not in skins and with a club, a club made of a stick with a big kno
at the end of it, and a spear and a shield. I think that I have put tha
aside. We think that we all have put those things aside, or are put
ting them aside, and that is why I am standing in the midst of yo
people today dressed in European clothes.[10]

"NOT SOLVED BY FEATHERS"

Somewhat in a similar vein were the remarks uttered b
Geronimo Martin, Navajo Indian, a student (now inter
preter) at a California Young Men's Christian Associatio
boys' campfire program:

Everywhere we Indians go you white boys ask us where ou
feather headdresses, our moccasins, and our "real Indian" costume
are. . . . Don't you know that those are the ways that our great
grandparents dressed a very long time ago? It is just as though whe
you should come to the reservation to visit us we Indians woul
ask you about your buckskin shirts, your flintlock muskets, an
your covered wagons. All those things belong *back in the past. Le
them stay there.* . . . We young Indians, who want to help ou

people, face some great problems. . . . We need your help. The problems we are facing *will never be solved by feathers!*

Does not this appeal call on the great body of churches throughout the country as never before to realize that not only Navajo youth but Indians elsewhere wish to be considered as friends and neighbors; that they covet the opportunity to know and to be known by other Americans, young and old alike, as fellow-Christians building a new world of mutual understanding and self-respect?

Speaking as an Indian, facing these same problems of Indian youth from a somewhat different angle, Louis Bruce, Jr., of Mohawk-Sioux descent, formerly Director of Indian Projects for the National Youth Administration in New York State, in addressing the annual meeting of the Indian Rights Association, said:

The future success and happiness of the Indian people depend upon their cooperation with and not their antagonism toward the people whom many older Indians see as usurpers. The task is, however, not alone with the red man. It is not to the white man's advantage that in his midst there are groups of economically dependent people who see him as an aggressor and one who takes unfair advantage. If the Indian is to change his outlook and reestablish his economic dignity, the white man must needs change his viewpoint and from his more advantageous position offer friendliness and encouragement.[11]

Thus we have recorded the considered and articulate expressions of some present-day Indian leaders who, while recognizing the cultural contribution of their people, also realize that each culture is a "mosaic of many cultures" and that their own future as well as that of their contemporary fellow-Americans cannot, to any significant extent, lie along aboriginal folkways; that the isolation policy is untenable for races as well as nations. They agree with Sir Austen Chamberlain that "none of us can find security in isolation," and subscribe to the words of the late Archbishop Söderblom, Primate of Sweden, when he said, "He who takes his stand on an isolation platform stands on a death platform." Certainly if the Indian is to hold the place of his own choosing in tomorrow's world, that choice will not be tribalism, segregation, and isolation.

THE CHRISTIAN GOAL

What does the church of Christ say to these things? The Christian goal, as has already been pointed out, is to make all nations of the earth one; the Christian standard recognizes no racial distinctions; segregation has no place, neither does isolation. Tribalism cannot save the American Indian; not by a withdrawal from the stream of American life nor in a back-to-the-reservation movement can racial salvation come.

The late Dr. George W. Hinman, long a student of Indian affairs, made this discerning comment: "The fundamental mistake in our early government policy toward the Indians was that they were subjugated instead of being assimilated." Continuing with special reference to early-day missionary endeavor, he said:

> Without definitely formulating a policy these Christian pioneers in the Indian country were actually practising the policy of Christian assimilation, working out a method by which whites and Indians could live together in harmony, mutually sharing in the benefits of the land and sharing also in the obligations of a Christian society. It has taken a long time for people generally to come to this point of view as the only real solution of our problem.[12]

THE CHURCH'S TASK AND THE NEW DAY

The church must continue to furnish the source of new life on new trails in this transition from the old to the new. While the day of missionary pioneering in the sense of blazing new trails through forest and across prairie has largely passed, neglected and partially occupied areas still beckon urgently for church extension in the primary and fundamental sense of that term. While the frontiers are indeed receding in the Indian country, still there are groups uncared for religiously. Specifically, these are largely to be found in such western states as Utah, Nevada, New Mexico, Arizona, and California as well as in the far stretches of northern Canada and Alaska. In some instances the difficulties in reaching these small and scattered bands are enormous. Probably an itinerant ministry of a new sort is needed. Furthermore, a pooling of personnel and funds on the part of boards and societies would be an immediate step in realizing the goal. Under this same heading should be added what someone has called the "burned-over fields," where at one time religious activities were going forward but now, because of retrenchment policies, the places have been abandoned.

It is fundamental that the church's mission to Indians or any similar minority group will depend upon the interpretation of missions in relation to people everywhere.[13] What shall we say of discrimination and segregation as they are still flagrantly practised against such groups? In addressing the Western Regional Conference of the National Fellowship of Indian Workers, held at Lake Tahoe, California, in August, 1940, the former Superintendent of the Sacramento Indian Agency stated: "Today in California an Indian is not welcome in most restaurants, he is shown to the rear seats in the gallery at cinemas although his ticket entitles him to a seat anywhere in the house. Hundreds of California Indians never have been within the doors of a white home." Then, turning to the group present, he asked the following pointed question: "I ask you who are church workers and missionaries, in how many white churches in California are Indians made welcome?" That the list of states and provinces might be considerably lengthened who will question? In the light of this and similar situations, who is prepared to deny that the church has countenanced segregation in various forms? Should not the church be the first rather than the last agency to abolish every vestige of racial discrimination in tomorrow's world?

ASSUMPTION OF OBLIGATIONS

In any discussion of the church's task and the Indian's part in a post-war world, the fact needs to be constantly reiterated that there can be no real freedom without the assumption of obligations. On the statue of General Giles Waldo Shurtleff of Oberlin College, the first Brigadier General in charge of Negro troops during the Civil War, there is inscribed, "Freedom cannot be given, it must be achieved." A similar sentiment was echoed by Rabbi Silver: "Freedom without the voluntary assumption of obligations, without sharing burdens and making sacrifices, is no freedom at all, but the sheerest anarchy." [14] Translated into present-day home mission terminology this means increasing self-support as well as self-government in Christian work among Indians. Cognizant of this need the Reverend David Owl, Cherokee, long-time missionary pastor to the Senecas in New York State, speaking on "Indian Views of Indian Missions" says:

> Scores of Indians of every tribe have been led to expect something for nothing rather than to earn their own living and to create

material and spiritual possessions for themselves. The fact that only a few Indian churches are self-sustaining and only a few are benevolent-minded is not wholly the fault of the Indians. Missionaries and government agents have sometimes encouraged them to "eat, sleep, and sit on the floor," by not giving them anything they could do well, or by not developing in them a sense of personal ambition to accomplish something difficult. Indians, like other peoples, catch a heavenly vision only as they begin with the improvement of the inner life. Every forward-looking Christian Indian is a personal testimony to the enduring worth and the uplifting influence of missions to Indians.[15]

A recent graduate of the Cook Christian Training School, Phoenix, Arizona, also sensing some of these disabilities, said in his Commencement address:

There can never be a real forward-looking church as long as we are willing to let the white people do all the work in it and furnish all the financial support for it. This is one of the weaknesses in many of the churches of our tribes.

The time has come now when the Indians should take on full responsibility of running and maintaining their own church and guiding it in the destiny which will bring the most promising results for the Indian people. It is time for the "leaders to take the lead."

We shall some day be able to do away with both religious and civil wardship and stand upon our own feet. This can only come as "the leaders take the lead, and the people give themselves willingly" to Christian citizenship.

Emphasizing how Indians respond to Christian stewardship, the late Dr. C. L. Hall, veteran missionary to the Fort Berthold (North Dakota) tribes, relates how one good preacher, handicapped by imperfect knowledge of English, interpreted a Bible passage: "One day he read the account of the woman who cast her all into the treasury. He had never heard of a mite, at least by that name; he read 'two mitts.' Then he preached an effective sermon on the consecration of a woman who had no money, but could embroider with beads or porcupine quills, and so made a fine pair of mitts for the Lord." [16]

That stimulating the Indian's willingness to work and to be thrifty is basic to self-support and self-respect is summed up tersely in a sentence that an Apache student in the first contingent of Indian protégés at Hampton Institute wrote home from there in the late 1870's: "I pray to God every day—and hoe onions." The first part showed that he had some appreciation of the humanities, that which contributes to self-respect, in that he had learned to link his own personality to the God who cares and provides; the second showed that in learning the dignity of labor he had already glimpsed the "work road" that leads to self-support.

Everywhere in the Indian mission field one senses the need of a more practical application of religion to the affairs of everyday life. This calls for an all-inclusive objective, that is, to make the realization of the kingdom of God on earth the aim. In the old life of the Indian his religion entered into everything, his planting, harvesting, feasting, recreation as well as ceremonials—all interests, including health and community life. If, then, this minority group is to be integrated into our body politic, the church must take the lead and increasingly minister to the full round of Indian needs, whether in camp, colony, or reservation, whether "checkerboarded" in the midst of a white, rural community, or within the confines of an organized village. Is there any cogent reason why an Indian mission may not become a center of good will to all sorts and conditions of men rather than serve on a level of segregation?

"THE MOST PERPLEXING ELEMENT"

Fifty years ago the then Commissioner of Indian Affairs, the Honorable T. J. Morgan, wrote in his annual report, "In our judgment of the Indian . . . we should remember that the most perplexing element in the problem is not the Indian, but the white man." Continuing, he launched into a tirade on some of the evils inflicted by bad white men on the red. Commenting similarly on certain types of the dominant race let loose on the aborigines, Dr. Warren K. Moorehead, former curator of the Department of American Archeology of Phillips Academy, and member at one time of the United States Board of Indian Commissioners, says:

> The powerful missionary organizations, comprising as they do hundreds of earnest workers, will accomplish much more for "Indian uplift" if they devote their energies to "pagan whites" as well as pagan Indians. The worst people I have met had white, and not red, skins. These men swarm about all Indian communities. Enough evidence against their character has been brought before the benevolent organizations and Washington to convince the most skeptical. Suppose the Indians of a certain region were found to be swindling each other, importing whiskey, gambling, stealing, and committing all sorts of crimes. Immediately half a dozen organizations would raise funds and send workers to "lead the pagans from darkness into light." It has been clearly shown that the worst elements of our white race are responsible for the deplorable condition of thousands of Indians. Yet I fail to observe any concerted effort to check this evil at its source.[17]

Written twenty-five years ago, this might with equal emphasis be cited as a scathing indictment of present-day conditions in certain parts of the Indian country.

A somewhat different point of view, though bearing on white populations adjacent to Indian reservations, is expressed by a field missionary in the following language: "Another important matter is the attitude of the local white churches in Indian communities. If the Christian people on the reservations could be helped to see their opportunity, it would wonderfully help the Indian's cause, and a campaign directed by the right people on all reservations might result in great good." [18] Today as never before these churches should realize that the Indians will be among them as neighbors in their communities and that at many points a Christian witness can be given right in the life of the congregation. Too often have they been regarded as objects of a separate mission endeavor by white people going into distant places to work among segregated Indians.

In fact, the present situation may very well call for a new type of pioneering. The feasibility of establishing demonstration centers over a period of years in strategic places where an all-around community program might be fostered under the auspices of Christian agencies should receive serious consideration.

COMPETITION MUST GIVE WAY TO COOPERATION

Again, if the Indian's part in tomorrow's world is to make for increasing participation in American church life, competition must give way to cooperation, which is just another way of saying that ecclesiastical barriers, often menacing in the past, must be broken down. That the Indian has but superficially grasped our historical denominational differences is evident from the names given to the various denominations. For example, the Roman Catholics are "long coats" or "drags his coat"; the Episcopalians are "white coats"; the Methodists, Congregationalists, and Presbyterians are "short coats" or "sprinklers"; while the Baptists are "ducks under the water"; and the Pentecostals are classified as "shouters" or "rollers."

In summing up what seemed to be "fundamental if the Christian religion is to be a factor in transforming Indian life and anchoring it in those ideals that spring out of direct and pronounced Christianity," an experienced field missionary includes the following:

> I would emphasize a more concentrated cooperative effort of religious organizations to bring the Indian life into regular contact with the fundamentals of our Christian religion, freed from those secondary controverted points of our faith out of which spring denominational rivalry and confusing differences in the Indian mind.[19]

While some progress in interdenominational cooperation may be recorded, such as religious education in Indian schools, the fellowship missionary conferences, and certain zoning arrangements worked out by denominational agencies in the field, nevertheless these "confusing differences in the Indian mind" brought about by sectarian rivalry need to be dealt with sympathetically but fearlessly in seeking to promote more adequate Indian participation in the church's program. Comity arrangements to prevent duplication of effort and overlapping in certain areas must still be worked out. Furthermore, there are certain questions that touch the life and work of the churches very intimately that can only be dealt with adequately on the basis of interdenominational cooperation. Among these one need only cite the liquor traffic, peyote, wardship, the exploitation of Indian women, just to mention a few. Beyond question the Archbishop of Canterbury struck a responsive chord in his first radio message to America, when he reminded his hearers that there is a great public ready to listen to what we say together, who do not pay any attention while we say it in separation.

PROVINCE OF THE CHRISTIAN MISSIONARY

But what of the Christian missionary in tomorrow's world? In this period of many changes and readjustments to new conditions, what is the province of the gospel messenger, whether of white or Indian ancestry? However sketchy and incomplete any attempt at outlining a modern missionary's task may be, there would be no question that it should include the following objectives:

1. A wise and sympathetic guide. It should be his function to explain the meaning of these new and strange relationships in which the Indian finds himself. Take citizenship, for example. What are the privileges, obligations, and immunities of citizenship? The reign of bullets has ceased; what about the reign of ballots? Should the wardship era end, what of the era of emancipation? What shall be the place of the Indian's choosing in the realm of civic responsibility?

2. Interpreter of the great mysteries of life to the Indian mind—those having to do with marriage, birth, baptism, and the last great mystery, death. These are a pastor's sacred duties to his people as shepherd to his flock. Since they partake of the eternal, they cannot be circumscribed by time or place; their significance is indeed timeless.

3. A wise adaptability. Someone has said that the prime requisites for the modern missionary to the Indian are a wise adaptability, a great patience, and a mighty hope. Certainly he must learn to know and appreciate the cultural background of those whom he seeks to serve as well as his people's capacity for knowledge, their thought life, and the conditions under which they live. A wise adaptability calls for a sympathetic understanding of the past, all that has entered into the varied inheritance of yesterday, plus the cumulative experiences that have ushered in the here and now with its

bristling problems crying for solution. A wise missionary will be quick to detect evidences of the "morning light" that is breaking through the darkness of superstition and prejudice, and to recognize that these sons of earth waking to "penitential tears" are indeed spiritual brothers and sisters—children of a loving, forgiving heavenly Father.

4. Stimulating self-help. The wise and forward-looking missionary will be vigilant to stimulate his people toward self-help. Instead of appealing to his supporting agency to furnish *all* the funds for a church building enterprise, for example, he will challenge the members "to show their faith by their works" by making an initial contribution toward it. A recent instance is that reported by a visiting missionary to a neighboring field:

> We saw the little chapel in process of construction. It is not a pretentious building and can never be. However, I am in hearty approval of the psychology used in letting it represent the work that comes out of the longings of the people themselves. Perhaps it is fair for me to say that I have spent seventeen years in the Ozark Hills under my own mission board. One of the most distressing things I've encountered in those years has been these poverty-stricken communities where the board or some fine sympathetic church did too much for a people. It can ruin and thwart and defeat every hope you have for them. May I say candidly and frankly that you people are doing the best that can be done for this small group of people when you help them, not to build pretentious buildings, but rather to realize some of the things they can do for themselves.
>
> This is a small group of people, poor people, who are getting, even slowly, a vision of the immense possibilities that the Christian life offers. To pick them out and give to them material blessings above their neighbors not so well situated would undoubtedly place them in something of an embarrassing position among their own people. I believe the whole enterprise has been carried so far in a

way that is helping to bring the Indian to a larger measure of self-respect, and the white people to something of like character.

5. Fellowship in the place of isolation. In the past there has been relatively little feeling of solidarity and unity on the part of Indian missionaries in their approach to the Indian field as a whole. Too often they have been isolated on the reservation of a particular tribe without knowing much, if anything, of methods and plans advantageously used elsewhere. As noted earlier, this isolation is gradually giving way to such "get-togethers" as those fostered by the National Fellowship of Indian Workers and similar organizations. Furthermore, fellowship in thought and prayer yields abundant harvest, for those who walk in the light of the Son of God speak a language all tribes can understand.

6. A long-time relationship. The Christian missionary enterprise to North American Indians can hardly take pride in the relatively large turnover of its personnel and the short-time relationship thus sustained to the work by a substantial majority. It takes a long time to become an effective Indian missionary. Anyone called and qualified for this service should consider it a life work. Practical experience and first-hand knowledge in actual field service are the things that count, and these cannot be obtained in a few years. This conviction was voiced at a conference of Indian workers in Canada in the following resolution: "That Indian missions shall not become a temporary resting place for men (or women) who are waiting for some station among white people to open, nor for men who are difficult to station." [20] That statement in a nutshell embodies truth too often suppressed heretofore in similar gatherings. Surely, as we face tomorrow's world, we can do no less than press for adequate training and a long-time relationship for our missionary personnel.

7. Exercising a cooperative spirit and approach with all xisting agencies for Indian uplift. This again calls for a wise daptability and great patience in the presence of different oints of view. It is no secret that missionaries and governnent officials have temperaments varying according to background and training. Said a former Commissioner of Indian Affairs: "I have known cases where the missionary and superntendent were of the same church denomination and yet ound it difficult to live peacefully together in a reservation hat covered more than 1,000,000 acres, for there was not oom enough for two temperamental men of opposite opinons to get together on any proposition."

The missionary enterprise in this new day must continue eeking to reach the unreached even as it did in its pioneer lays, never losing sight of its distinctive function to propagate the gospel but with an ever present readiness for change ccording to changing needs; in short, a program that changes ttitudes rather than serving as an end product.

That is to say, the home missionary enterprise must not be ontent with institutions that seem sufficient within themelves. The Roman Catholic church in Latin American counries has often fostered Indian missions that might be termed slands of isolation, the idea being that the Indians gathered vithin the mission compound and guarded from outside conacts would thus become self-sufficient. But history records he inevitable breakdown of this sort of isolationism. Even a nission school, essential and highly desirable in its place, may utgrow its usefulness. "New occasions teach new duties, ime makes ancient good uncouth."

LEAVEN OF CHRISTIANITY INDISPENSABLE

In the last analysis, if the Indian is to occupy his rightful place in tomorrow's world, he will need the leavening influence of Christianity as never before. In amplifying this thought a missionary phrased it as follows:

> I do not believe that, generally, among the churches, there has been enough intelligent presentation of the necessity of Christianizing the Indian in order that he may succeed otherwise. While we believe that for him to succeed as a Christian he must have the material necessities in prosperity (or, as often so depicted), we likewise believe that he will not, as a whole, prosper without the leaven of Christianity.[21]

In underscoring the foregoing we also do well to remind ourselves of the vitality and persistence of the Christian missionary motive so well expressed by Warneck:

> The victorious power of the Christian faith reveals itself in that the gospel triumphs because of its message of certainty, it gives stability, it proclaims a personal living God, it brings salvation, it presents God's love which gave, it creates morality in its truest sense, it brings the hope of everlasting life.[22]

Finally, the Cross must be our uniting symbol in the postwar world. We must put love in the place of hate, fellowship in the place of isolation, cooperation in the place of competition. Shall we not take our stand under the banner of the Cross as we consider the part our Indian brother in company with all who name the name of Christ are to bear in tomorrow's world?

REFERENCES

1. "Shall the Indian Be Kept Indian?" in *The Rotarian*, May, 1938 p. 62.
2. *Indians at Work*, January, 1936, p. 24.

3. Quoted in "The Government's New Indian Policy," *Missionary Review of the World*, April, 1934, p. 184.
4. "Indian Education: Suggestions for Improving the Prevailing System," presented to the Minister of Mines and Resources, November 21, 1938.
5. In conversation with author.
6. Proceedings of meeting held by Senator Elmer Thomas with the Indians of the Kiowa Agency at Anadarko, Oklahoma, October 23, 1934, p. 25.
7. Report of May 15, 1934, to American Indian Defense Association.
8. Letter to author on proposed Indian legislation.
9. From lecture notes taken December 1, 1933, at Albuquerque, New Mexico.
10. From an address at the Pima Day Schools, Sacaton, Arizona, March 28, 1940.
11. *Indian Truth*, January, 1940, Vol. 17, No. 1, p. 2.
12. *The American Indian and Christian Missions*, by George W. Hinman, pp. 41, 164. New York, Fleming H. Revell Co., 1933.
13. Miss Thelma Stevens of the Methodist Board of Missions, Woman's Division of Christian Service, developed this thought in her discussion of minority groups, at the Home Missions Council, Cleveland, Ohio, December, 1942.
14. *Religion in a Changing World*, by Abba Hiller Silver. New York, Harper & Brothers, 1930.
15. *Missionary Review of the World*, July-August, 1932, p. 413.
16. Quoted in *The Word Carrier*, Santee, Nebraska, January, 1918.
17. *The American Indian*, by Warren K. Moorehead, p. 289. Andover, The Andover Press, 1914.
18. Quoted in "Christian Missions among the American Indians," Bulletin No. 280, Board of Indian Commissioners, p. 13.
19. *Ibid.*, p. 10.
20. *One Hundred Years of Methodist Missions*, p. 254.
21. Statement to author.
22. Quoted in *Sanningsstrålar av K. E. Laman*, p. 89. Stockholm, Sv. Missionsförbundets Förlag, 1923.

HIGHLIGHTS FROM THE CHRONOLOGY OF PROTESTANT MISSIONS AMONG NORTH AMERICAN INDIANS

1619 Council of Jamestown, Va., voted "to educate Indian children in religion a civil course of life and some useful trade"; Henrico College was probably the school designated.

1635 Roger Williams preached to the Wampanoag and Narragansett Indians

1638 Settlement of Swedes in Delaware. The Rev. Johan Campanius first pastor and missionary; later translated Lutheran catechism into Indian tongue.

1643 First Protestant mission for Indians established by Thomas Mayhew at Martha's Vineyard.

1646 John Eliot, the "Apostle to the Indians," began work among New England tribes.

1649 Corporation for the Propagation of the Gospel among the Indians of New England established in London.

1671 George Fox of the Society of Friends preached to Indians of Atlantic seaboard.

1681 First Indian minister, Daniel Takawambpait, ordained at Natick.

1697 A school for Indians in connection with William and Mary College opened at Williamsburg, Va.

1701 Society for the Propagation of the Gospel in Foreign Parts (S. P. G.) organized. Episcopalians launched work among Iroquois in New York State.

1735 Moravians opened their Georgia mission.
Friends sent missionaries to the Cherokees in North Carolina.
Wesleyans also started work among Cherokees.

1740 The Moravians established missions among Eastern tribes and in 174[illegible] organized The Society of the United Brethren for Propagating the Gospel among the Heathen.

1746 David Brainerd began work among the Munsees in New Jersey.

1754 Moor's Indian Charity School (later Dartmouth College) opened at Lebanon, Conn., by Eleazer Wheelock.

1760 The Church of England in Canada working among the Indians of the Maritime Provinces.

1785 First Anglican church in upper Canada built; work among Mohawks sponsored by the Corporation for the Propagation of the Gospel among the Indians of New England; Mohawk Institute, near Brantfort, Ont., still receives support from S. P. G.
Methodists began work among Mohawks along Grant River, Ont., in post-Revolutionary period.

1787 The Society for Propagating the Gospel among the Indians and Others in North America incorporated at Boston; known as "the oldest incorporated missionary society in America."

1803 Nathan Banks, Methodist, began preaching to the Delawares.

1805 The New York Missionary Society began work among the Five Nations, later turning missions over to the Presbyterians.

1810 The American Board of Commissioners for Foreign Missions (A.B.C.F.M.) organized under auspices of Congregational, Presbyterian, and Reformed churches; initiated missions and schools among many tribes during seven decades.

1816 Methodist mission work, under the Rev. John Stewart, launched among Wyandots near Sandusky, Ohio.
Episcopalians founded a mission among Oneidas.

1818 The Rev. Isaac McCoy, Baptist, began eventful career as missionary, serving nearly thirty years.

1820 The Rev. John West, known as the founder of the Indian boarding school system, sent as chaplain to Red River Settlement (now Winnipeg) by the Hudson's Bay Company.

1821 Sequoya invented Cherokee alphabet of eighty-six characters.

1826 First regularly appointed missionary of Canadian Methodism, Edgerton Ryerson, began work at Credit Mission in Ontario.

1830 Six Nations Temperance League organized by the Iroquois.

1831 Indian delegation at St. Louis in search for "the white man's book of heaven."

1834 Dakota (Sioux) Mission opened by the Rev. Thomas S. Williamson near Lac Qui Parle, Minn.; he was joined in 1837 by the Rev. Stephen Return Riggs.
Jason Lee, Methodist, founded first mission in Pacific Northwest, near Ft. Vancouver, Wash.

1835 Dr. Marcus Whitman launched far-reaching missionary work in Pacific Northwest together with the Rev. H. H. Spalding and Samuel Parker.

1836 The Rev. James Evans, in western Canada, invented Cree syllabic system for translation; still in use.

1840 Missionary work under Church of England auspices extended to Munceys, Oneidas, Chippewas, and Pottawatomies on Thames River, Ont.

1846 American Missionary Association organized; in 1883 took over Indian work of A.B.C.F.M.

1847 Evangelical Lutheran Mission Society of Dresden, Germany, established a mission among Chippewas in lower Michigan, later extending their efforts to Apaches in Arizona.

1849 Muncie Institute, now known as the Mt. Elgin Residential School, founded under Canadian Methodist auspices. Operated at present in cooperation with government.

1857 Coming of William Duncan of Metlakatla fame to Port Simpson, B. C. William Henry Pierce of Tsimshian tribe began preparation for missionary work.

1860 Bishop H. B. Whipple, of the Protestant Episcopal Church, opened a mission among Santee Sioux in Redwood, Minn.

1863 Bishop W. C. Bompas began a ministry of forty-three years among tribes in the Prairie Provinces.

1865 The Rev. W. W. Kirkly carried the gospel within the Arctic Circle.

1866 The Rev. James Nisbet (Presbyterian) launched work among the Crees on Saskatchewan River near present site of Prince Albert.
Miss Lucy Baker, credited with being first woman teacher, sent by Presbyterians to Canadian Indians.
United Presbyterians opened work on Warm Springs Reservation in Oregon.

1870 Experiment in assigning Indian agencies to denominational oversight launched.
First Protestant work in Arizona started by Charles H. Cook; taken over in 1878 by Presbyterians.
First appropriation by Canadian government for Indian education.

1873 Bishop William H. Hare, Episcopalian, launched far-reaching work of Protestant Episcopal Church among the Sioux in the Dakotas.

1874 Women's Missionary Society of Presbyterian Church, organized in Montreal in 1864, began work among Indians. Today is responsible for several mission schools, residential and day, in western Ontario, Manitoba, and Saskatchewan.

1878 Reformed Church in the United States began work among Winnebagos of Wisconsin.

1879 Bacone College, now located near Muskogee, Okla., opened by Baptists. Indian Young Men's Christian Association organized at Flandreau, S. D.

1880 National Indian Association organized.
The Haidas of Queen Charlotte Islands received the gospel.

1881 Chief Joseph of Oka band, Quebec, translated portions of New Testament into Iroquois.

1884 Norwegian Evangelical Lutheran Church established a mission boarding school at Wittenberg, Wis.

1889 First medical missionary at Port Simpson, B. C.; first hospital 1892.
Moravians launched work among Mission Indians near Banning, Calif.

1891 Mission school among the Navajos opened on San Juan River by Methodists; later moved to Farmington, N. M.

1892 First Young Women's Christian Association in Indian schools organized.
Danish Lutheran Mission established at Oaks, Okla.

1894 Oklahoma Presbyterian College, located at Durant, founded.
Evangelical Lutheran Church (Synod of Wisconsin) started work among Apaches in Arizona.
Baptists started work among Hopis near Toreva, Ariz.

1895 Episcopalians and Methodists launched work among Paiutes of Nevada, at Pyramid Lake and Walker River respectively.
Colony, Okla., Reformed Church mission among Cheyennes and Arapahos opened.

1897 Christian Reformed Mission among Zuñis in New Mexico launched.

1905 Southern Baptists began work among the Osages; the following year extended their mission to the Pawnees in Oklahoma.

1907 Women's Board of Domestic Missions of the Reformed Church in America opened mission among Mescalero Apaches in New Mexico.

1908 The Home Missions Council organized and in 1910 the Council of Women for Home Missions. Through their Committee on Indian Missions interdenominational work in government non-reservation schools opened in 1919.

1919 First interdenominational missionary conference held at Wichita, Kan.
American Indian survey launched under the Inter-Church World Movement and completed in 1922 under the Institute for Social and Religious Research.

1920 National Indian Association began work with Rocky Boy's Band, Montana; later this was turned over to the United Lutheran Church.
United Christian Missionary Society established mission dormitory on the Yakima reservation, Washington.

1935 National Fellowship of Indian Workers organized at Madison, Wis.; regional conferences established in 1937; first national conference at Farmington, N. M., 1941.

A SELECTED READING LIST

THERE is a very wide range of literature both on the general history and description of the North American Indians as well as on the work of Christian missions. It has not been possible to cite here more than a very brief selection of titles. For the most part those listed are of fairly recent date, easily available and moderate in price. Some older books of special value for reference have been included even though out of print and are marked O. P. Many of these are available even in small libraries. Most libraries in the United States and Canada can supply works on the Indians of their surrounding regions. These collections are often very rich in anthropology, fiction, and biography, and in personal memoirs of the pioneering period, and should be drawn upon to supplement this list.

The views of the authors represented here are not necessarily in harmony with those of the author of this book.

Leaders of adult groups studying this subject will find a helpful guide, based primarily on this book, in the pamphlet entitled "Discussion and Program Suggestions for Adults on the American Indian," by Bertha M. Eckert. Published by Friendship Press, New York, it is available through denominational literature headquarters, price 25 cents.

General Backgrounds and History

BEAVER, KINGS AND CABINS, by Constance L. Skinner. New York, The Macmillan Co., 1933. $2.75. History of the fur trade of the Pacific Northwest.

CHANGING INDIAN, THE, edited by Oliver La Farge. Norman, University of Oklahoma Press, 1942. $2.00. A symposium on the present status of the Indian.

CONTINENT LOST, A CIVILIZATION WON, A, by Jay P. Kinney. Baltimore, Johns Hopkins Press, 1937. $4.00. A reference book on land policy.

HISTORY OF THE AMERICAN FRONTIER, 1763-1893, by Frederic L. Paxson. Boston, Houghton Mifflin Co., 1924. $2.75. Indians and pioneers figure in this study.

INDIAN AGENTS OF THE OLD FRONTIER, by Flora Warren Seymour. New York, D. Appleton-Century Co., 1941. $3.50. In presenting Indian agents of the frontier, this volume depicts Indian history from the Civil War to the 1920's.

INDIAN EXPERIENCES, by DeCost Smith. Caldwell, Idaho, The Caxton Printers, 1943. $4.00. An accurate portrayal by an artist of life among the Sioux Indians of Dakota in the early years of this century.

"Indian Wardship." New York, Home Missions Council, 1943. 15 cents. A detailed statement outlining the history of wardship from 1831 to the present.

INDIANS ARE PEOPLE, TOO, by Ruth Muskrat Bronson. New York, Friendship Press, 1944. Cloth $1.00; paper 60 cents. An Indian leader of wide experience among the youth of her people tells how Indian Americans view their past and interprets their adjustment to the changes of today.

MY FRIEND THE INDIAN, by James McLaughlin. Boston, Houghton Mifflin Co., 1910. $4.00. Reminiscences from a lifetime of acquaintance with Indian tribes, especially the Sioux.

NORTH AMERICAN INDIAN TODAY, THE, edited by Charles T. Loram and T. F. McIlwraith. Toronto, University of Toronto Press, 1943. $3.00. One of the most important recent volumes for general background. A report of the University of Toronto-Yale University Seminar Conference, held at Toronto, September, 1939.

OFFICE OF INDIAN AFFAIRS, THE, by Laurence F. Schmeckebier. Baltimore, Johns Hopkins Press, 1927. $3.00. Useful reference on the history and scope of the Indian Office.

"Peyote Intoxication—Some Psychological Aspects of the Peyote Rite," by Drs. Bromberg and Tranter in *The Journal of Nervous and Mental Disease,* May, 1943. Available, together with "Some Pertinent Comments," by Philip M. Riley, from Home Missions Council, New York. 5 cents for both.

PROBLEM OF INDIAN ADMINISTRATION, THE, by Lewis Meriam and associates. Baltimore, Johns Hopkins Press, 1928. $5.00. A survey of the United States Indian field service.

STORY OF THE RED MAN, THE, by Flora Warren Seymour. Boston, Longmans, Green and Co., 1929. (O. P.) A graphic account of Indian life, past and present.

TWENTIETH CENTURY INDIANS, by Frances Cooke MacGregor. New York, G. P. Putnam's Sons, 1941. $3.00. A survey of Indian life and culture today, presented through photographs and text.

UNCLE SAM'S STEPCHILDREN, by Loring Benson Priest. New Brunswick, Rutgers University Press, 1942. $3.75. A study of the United States Indian policy, 1865-1887.

WE CALLED THEM INDIANS, by Flora Warren Seymour. New York, D. Appleton-Century Co., 1940. $2.00. Brief history of the Indians of the United States.

"What About Peyote?" New York, Home Missions Council, 1941. Free. Contains excerpts from leading authorities.

Indian Life, Cultures, and Crafts

AMERICAN INDIAN, THE, by Clark Wissler. Third edition. New York, Oxford University Press, 1938. $3.75. An introduction to the anthropology of the New World.

AMERICAN INDIANS AND THEIR MUSIC, by Frances Densmore. New York, Womans Press, 1926. $1.00. An excellent resource on history, customs, and music.

BOOK OF INDIAN CRAFTS AND INDIAN LORE, by Julian H. Salomon. New York, Harper & Brothers, 1928. $3.50. Recognized as a standard.

HE WHO ALWAYS WINS, by Richard H. Pousma. Grand Rapids, Wm. B. Eerdmans Publishing Co., 1934. $1.00. Navajo folk tales gathered by a missionary doctor.

INDIAN HOW BOOK, THE, by Arthur C. Parker. Garden City, Doubleday, Doran & Co., 1927. $2.50. An Indian tells how his people did things in camp and on the trail.

INDIANS OF THE UNITED STATES, by Clark Wissler. Garden City, Doubleday, Doran & Co., 1941. $3.75. Excellent anthropological study, especially of Siouan tribes.

"Ojibway Crafts," by Carrie A. Lyford. Published by Education Division, United States Indian Service; available from Haskell Institute, Lawrence, Kansas. 50 cents. Portrays faithfully the Ojibway patterns in craftsmanship.

POTTERY OF THE AMERICAN INDIANS, by Helen E. Stiles. New York, E. P. Dutton & Co., 1939. $2.50.

"Quill and Beadwork of the Western Sioux," by Carrie A. Lyford. Published by Education Division, United States Indian Service; available from Haskell Institute, Lawrence, Kansas. 50 cents.

SPEAKING OF INDIANS, by Ella C. Deloria. New York, Friendship Press, 1944. Cloth $1.00; paper 60 cents. An Indian anthropologist unfolds the background of her people, and tells of their changing life today in school, church, and community.

Biography

AMERICAN: THE LIFE STORY OF A GREAT INDIAN, by Frank B. Linderman. New York, The John Day Co., 1930. $3.50. Life story of Plenty-coups, Chief of the Crows.

APACHE AGENT, by Woodworth Clum. Boston, Houghton Mifflin Co., 1936. $3.00. Story of John P. Clum, a boy agent of the seventies.

BLACK ELK SPEAKS, by John G. Neihardt. New York, William Morrow & Co., 1932. (O. P.) An old Sioux's life story as told to the poet.

CHEROKEE MESSENGER, by Althea Bass. Norman, University of Oklahoma Press, 1936. $3.00. Biography of Samuel Worcester.

CIVILIZATION, by Thomas Wildcat Alford. Norman, University of Oklahoma Press, 1936. $2.50. A Shawnee tells the story of his life.

CRASHING THUNDER, by Paul Radin. New York, D. Appleton-Century Co., 1926. (O. P.) Life Story of a Winnebago Indian.

ELIAS BOUDINOT, CHEROKEE, AND HIS AMERICA, by Ralph Henry Gabriel. Norman, University of Oklahoma Press, 1941. $2.00. Life story of Elias Boudinot on the basis of a collection of letters. Teacher, editor, leader, he was one of the important figures in the tragic drama of the Cherokee Indians in their association and conflict with the white conquerors.

FROM THE DEEP WOODS TO CIVILIZATION, by Charles A. Eastman. Boston, Little, Brown and Co., 1916. (O. P.) Chapters in the autobiography of an Indian.

HENRY HARMON SPALDING, by Clifford Merrill Drury. Caldwell, Idaho, The Caxton Printers, 1936. $3.00. How civilization and Christianity came to the Nez Percés.

MARCUS WHITMAN, M.D., by Clifford Merrill Drury. Caldwell, Idaho, The Caxton Printers, 1937. $5.00. A faithful record of the pioneer missionary doctor.

MEMORIES OF A WHITE CROW INDIAN (Thomas Leforge), told by Thomas B. Marquis. New York, The Century Co., 1928. (O. P.) Life story of a man who lived among the Crows.

MY PEOPLE, THE SIOUX, by Luther Standingbear. Boston, Houghton Mifflin Co., 1928. $4.00. A picturesque tale of an important prairie tribe.

PRATT: THE RED MAN'S MOSES, by Elaine Goodale Eastman. Norman, University of Oklahoma Press, 1935. $3.00. Story of the founder of Carlisle.

SACAJAWEA OF THE SHOSHONES, by Della Gould Emmons. Portland, Oregon, Binfords & Mort, 1943. $2.50. The life story of the Lewis and Clark guide told in novel form.

TECUMSEH AND HIS TIMES, by John M. Oskison. New York, G. P. Putnam's Sons, 1938. $2.75. Story of an Indian warrior by a part-Cherokee.

WAH' KON-TAH, by John Joseph Mathews. Norman, University of Oklahoma Press, 1932. $1.00. Somewhat fictionized story of a Quaker agent to the Osages by an Osage who was a Rhodes Scholar.

WE MUST MARCH, by Honoré Willsie Morrow. New York, Frederick A. Stokes Co., 1925. (O. P.) A story of Marcus Whitman among Northwestern Indians.

WOMEN OF TRAIL AND WIGWAM, by Flora Warren Seymour. New York, The Woman's Press, 1930. 75 cents. Stories of notable Indian women.

The Church and Its Missions

AMERICAN INDIAN AND CHRISTIAN MISSIONS, THE, by George W. Hinman. New York, Fleming H. Revell Co., 1933. (O. P.) A series of studies concerning missions among American Indians.

FACING THE FUTURE IN INDIAN MISSIONS, by Lewis Meriam and George W. Hinman. New York, Friendship Press, 1932. Cloth 50 cents; paper 25 cents.

HANDBOOK FOR MISSIONARY WORKERS AMONG THE AMERICAN INDIANS, A, by G. E. E. Lindquist. New York, Home Missions

Council, 1932. (O. P.) Especially designed for new recruits entering missionary service.

INASMUCH, by S. Gould. Toronto, The Missionary Society of the Church of England in Canada, 1917. Sketches of the beginnings of the Church of England in Canada in relation to the Indian and Eskimo races.

INDIAN AMERICANS, by Winifred Hulbert. New York, Friendship Press, 1932. (O. P.)

JESUS ROAD AND THE RED MAN, THE, by G. E. E. Lindquist. New York, Fleming H. Revell Co., 1929. (O. P.) Studies of the "Jesus Road" in relation to American Indians.

LIGHTS AND SHADOWS OF A LONG EPISCOPATE, by Bishop H. B. Whipple. New York, The Macmillan Co., 1902. (O. P.) Early-day efforts among the Chippewas in the Northwest.

MISSIONARY EXPLORERS AMONG THE AMERICAN INDIANS, edited by Mary Gay Humphreys. New York, Charles Scribner's Sons, 1913. (O. P.)

NEZ PERCÉS SINCE LEWIS AND CLARK, THE, by Kate C. McBeth. New York, Fleming H. Revell Co., 1908. (O. P.)

ONE HUNDRED YEARS OF CANADIAN METHODIST MISSIONS, by Mrs. Frederick C. Stephenson. Toronto, Young People's Forward Movement, 1925. Includes the story of the Indian missions of the Canadian Methodists in the years prior to formation of the United Church of Canada.

RED MAN IN THE UNITED STATES, THE, by G. E. E. Lindquist. New York, George H. Doran Co., 1923. (O. P.) Location and religious status of all tribes.

"Stewards of a Goodly Heritage," edited by H. Walsh. Toronto, The Joint Committee on Summer Schools and Institutes of the Church of England in Canada, 1934. 50 cents. A survey of the Church of England's mission fields in Canada.

"This Is the Indian," by Earle F. Dexter. New York, Friendship Press, 1944. 25 cents. A pictorial pamphlet of Indians and Indian missions in the United States, past and present.

TORCHLIGHTS TO THE CHEROKEES: THE BRAINERD MISSION, by Robert Sparks Walker. New York, The Macmillan Co., 1931. (O. P.) Story of the Brainerd mission.

INDEX